THE STORY OF
ZOOM

The Triumphs and Trials of a Video Conferencing Powerhouse

FRANCIS FORD

Copyright Notice

This book is copyrighted in 2019-2024 by Dan & Elbert Associates.

All rights reserved.
Its content may not be copied or duplicated in part or whole by any means without express prior agreement in writing

TABLE OF CONTENTS

Introduction	5
Chapter 1: New Vision in Communication	7
Chapter 2: The Birth of Zoom	21
Chapter 3: Breaking into a Crowded Market	31
Chapter 4: The Rise of Zoom	43
Chapter 5: From Tool to Verb: The Pandemic Era	49
Chapter 6: Growing Pains	55
Chapter 7: The Cultural Phenomenon	63
Chapter 8: The Road to Innovation	69
Chapter 9: Challenges and Critiques	75
Chapter 10: The Legacy of Zoom	87
Conclusion	93

Introduction

In a world constantly shaped by innovation, few technologies manage to transcend their functional purpose and become integral to the way people live, work, and connect. Zoom is one such phenomenon. What began as a niche tool for video conferencing quietly grew into a cultural and technological revolution, reshaping the norms of communication and altering the fabric of global interaction. Its journey from a Silicon Valley startup to a household name is a story of vision, determination, and the relentless pursuit of simplicity in a complex world. More than a tool, Zoom became a symbol of resilience and adaptability in the face of unprecedented challenges, touching lives across continents and industries.

This book chronicles the rise of Zoom, offering a deep dive into the factors that propelled its meteoric success and exploring the profound impact it has had on society. At its heart is the story of Eric Yuan, a visionary leader whose journey from a small town in China to the forefront of global innovation exemplifies the power of perseverance and empathy. But Zoom's story is not just about one man or one company—it is about how technology can bridge divides, democratize opportunities, and connect a fragmented world.

The narrative unfolds against the backdrop of a rapidly changing technological landscape, where competition is fierce and the demands of users evolve at lightning speed. From its early days navigating a crowded market dominated by giants like Skype and Google to its pivotal role during the COVID-19 pandemic, Zoom's ascent reflects a perfect alignment of innovation, timing, and a deep understanding of human needs. Yet, this is also a story of growing pains—of grappling with security flaws, ethical dilemmas, and the pressures of scaling overnight to meet the demands of a world in crisis.

This book is not merely a recounting of Zoom's history but an exploration of its cultural, social, and economic legacy. It examines how Zoom transformed businesses, revolutionized education, and redefined personal connections, leaving an indelible mark on how people perceive and use technology. It also delves into the challenges that accompanied this transformation, offering a nuanced perspective on what it means to build and sustain a technology that impacts millions.

Whether you are a tech enthusiast, a business leader, or someone curious about the forces shaping modern communication, this book invites you to reflect on the ways innovation influences our lives. It is a story of connection—not just between people and technology but between vision and execution, challenges and triumphs, and the past and future of human interaction. Zoom's journey is far from over, but its legacy is already being written in the way we meet, collaborate, and stay close in an ever-expanding digital world.

Chapter 1:
New Vision in Communication

Eric Yuan's journey traces its roots to Tai'an, a serene city located at the foot of Mount Tai in China's Shandong Province. Born in 1970 to parents who worked as mining engineers, Yuan grew up in an environment shaped by structure, discipline, and an emphasis on diligence. His parents instilled in him the values of persistence and hard work, qualities essential for navigating the challenges of life in a city with a largely industrial economy. Tai'an, while not a hub of technological innovation, provided Yuan with a quiet backdrop to cultivate his early interests. It was here that his natural curiosity about the world around him began to take shape. Unlike the prototypical technology prodigies who start coding in their early years, Yuan's fascination with technology emerged in subtler, more personal ways, shaped by his surroundings and relationships.

As a teenager, Yuan's first significant brush with problem-solving came from a deeply personal place: the desire to stay connected with his long-distance girlfriend, who lived hundreds of miles away. In an era before cell phones, email, or video communication, this posed a considerable challenge. Conversations were limited to infrequent letters and rare phone calls, leaving Yuan searching for better ways to bridge the gap. Although the technological solutions he dreamed of were decades away from realization, this desire to overcome distance planted a seed in his mind. It was less about the technology itself and more about what it could achieve—bringing people closer and solving real-world problems. Even at a young age, Yuan was not just interested in understanding how things worked but in imagining what could be created to improve lives.

Tai'an's industrial and modestly paced life meant that access to cutting-edge technology was limited, but this didn't stifle Yuan's ambition. In fact, the constraints likely fueled his creativity, as he had to think beyond the resources available to him. Yuan dreamed not in the abstract but with a clear goal: to engineer solutions that mattered. He was fascinated by the possibilities of creation, even if he couldn't yet articulate the tools he would need to build what he envisioned. It wasn't simply about learning to use technology; it was about using technology as a means to an end—one that brought meaning and connection to human interactions.

This early experience also reflected Yuan's empathy, a characteristic that would define his approach to leadership and innovation later in life. His desire to solve problems wasn't purely technical but rooted in a personal understanding of human needs. The frustration of being unable to connect with someone he cared about became a driving force that shaped his worldview. Yuan didn't merely dream of personal success; he dreamed of creating systems that could make life better for others, even if he didn't yet know how.

While many inventors and innovators are driven by a desire to achieve fame or recognition, Yuan's motivation was distinctly humanistic from the beginning. It was this focus on people rather than technology for its own sake that set him apart, even in his formative years. Though the tools to address the challenges he encountered as a teenager wouldn't materialize until much later, the seed had been planted. Yuan began to imagine a world where technology wasn't just a tool for productivity but a bridge that connected people, regardless of distance or circumstance.

This foundational period in Tai'an was crucial in shaping Yuan's character and aspirations. It was a place that nurtured his imagination while grounding him in the values of hard work and persistence. These early experiences of problem-solving, combined with a deep sense of empathy, would become the bedrock upon which Yuan would build his future. Even as his path took him far from his hometown, the lessons learned in Tai'an would remain with him, guiding his vision to create tools that could truly transform human interaction.

The Seeds of Ambition: Education and Early Inspiration

As China entered a period of rapid modernization in the late 20th century, the nation's expanding economy and growing emphasis on technological development opened new doors for ambitious students. Eric Yuan was among those who recognized these opportunities and seized them with characteristic determination. His aptitude for mathematics and science was evident early on, setting him apart from his peers and earning him a place at Shandong University of Science and Technology. Here, he pursued a degree in applied mathematics with a focus on computer applications, a discipline that bridged his logical acumen with his growing fascination for technology. It was during these years that Yuan encountered programming for the first time, an experience that would change the trajectory of his life. Learning to write code revealed to him the immense potential of software to transform industries and solve complex problems, igniting a passion that would define his career.

However, Yuan's aspirations were never confined to the boundaries of his home country. While China's modernization provided new opportunities, it was the stories of Silicon Valley that truly captured his imagination. In the 1980s and 1990s, Silicon Valley was synonymous with innovation, a place where bold ideas were turning into groundbreaking technologies that shaped the world. Yuan was fascinated by tales of young engineers and entrepreneurs who defied odds to revolutionize the tech landscape, creating a cultural and technological shift that rippled across the globe. To Yuan, Silicon Valley represented not just a physical destination but a vision of what was possible when creativity met opportunity. The dream of contributing to this ecosystem began to take root in his mind, providing a sense of purpose that extended beyond his academic studies.

While Yuan's passion for technology grew, he remained deeply connected to his family and their values. In deference to their legacy as mining engineers, he pursued a master's degree in mining engineering, a field that aligned with his parents' profession. This decision reflected Yuan's respect for tradition and his sense of duty to his family, even as his heart was increasingly drawn toward the possibilities of the digital age. It was a delicate balancing act, blending the expectations of his upbringing with his personal aspirations. Yet, even as he studied mining, his thoughts were increasingly consumed by the burgeoning field of technology, particularly the revolutionary potential of the internet.

The early 1990s marked the dawn of the internet revolution, a phenomenon that captivated the world with its promise of unprecedented connectivity and innovation. Yuan, like many of his generation, recognized the transformative potential of this new medium. It was a period of rapid change, where traditional industries were beginning to adapt to digital advancements, and entirely new markets were emerging. Yuan was acutely aware that this was a pivotal moment in history, one that required visionaries to step forward and shape the future. For him, the dream of Silicon Valley transitioned from an abstract fascination to a concrete goal: to become a part of the epicenter of global innovation.

This dream was not merely about personal achievement; it was rooted in Yuan's desire to contribute meaningfully to the world. He envisioned himself working on projects that could revolutionize industries and improve lives, driven by his belief in technology as a force for positive change. Silicon Valley represented the ultimate stage for turning these aspirations into reality, a place where ideas flourished and innovation was celebrated. For Yuan, the path to realizing his vision was clear: he needed to find a way to reach Silicon Valley, to immerse himself in its culture, and to learn from its pioneers.

This period of Yuan's life was characterized by a duality—he honored his family's professional legacy while simultaneously nurturing his own ambitions. It was a testament to his ability to reconcile tradition with innovation, a skill that would serve him well in the years to come. Yuan's focus on his studies and his growing fascination with the possibilities of technology set the foundation for what would become an extraordinary journey. His dream of Silicon Valley was not merely a personal aspiration but a reflection of his belief in the transformative power of technology to bridge gaps and create opportunities. This vision would propel him forward, driving him to overcome significant obstacles in his pursuit of a future that, at the time, seemed distant but was ultimately within his grasp.

A Relentless Pursuit: Overcoming Visa Denials
Yuan's dream of reaching Silicon Valley, the hub of technological innovation and entrepreneurial success, proved to be an arduous journey. The path was strewn with obstacles, the most daunting of which was gaining entry into the United States. In the 1990s, as he set his sights on becoming part of the burgeoning tech revolution, Yuan encountered an unexpected roadblock: repeated denials of his U.S. visa applications. Over the course of two years, he applied nine times, and each time he was met with rejection. For many, this string of setbacks might have signaled the end of their ambition, a discouraging barrier too formidable to overcome. However, for Yuan, each denial only deepened his resolve and sharpened his focus.

What drove Yuan to persevere in the face of such relentless rejection was not merely the lure of Silicon Valley's promise but a deeply ingrained belief in the potential of what he could contribute. To him, the journey was about more than personal advancement; it was about the opportunity to be part of a transformative wave of technological innovation. Yuan envisioned himself working on groundbreaking projects that would bridge distances and improve lives, and he refused to let temporary obstacles derail this vision. His determination was rooted in a conviction that the struggles he faced were a necessary step toward achieving something greater than himself.

The experience of repeatedly applying for a visa became a test of Yuan's character. Each rejection was a blow, but it also became a lesson in resilience. Yuan approached the process not with frustration but with a problem-solver's mindset, treating each setback as an opportunity to refine his approach. He exemplified an unwavering focus on the larger goal, a quality that would later define his leadership style and his ability to guide his team through challenges. Yuan's persistence during this period was a testament to his ability to remain steadfast in the face of adversity, a trait that would serve him well as he navigated the competitive and unpredictable world of technology startups.

Finally, on his tenth attempt, Yuan's application was approved. This moment was more than a procedural success; it was a defining milestone in his life, marking the culmination of years of persistence and belief in his vision. For Yuan, stepping onto U.S. soil was not just the beginning of a new chapter but a validation of his journey and the sacrifices he had made along the way. It underscored the principle that determination and grit could overcome even the most formidable barriers.

Yuan's visa approval was a turning point, but it also highlighted the strength of his character. It was not just about gaining entry to the United States; it was about what that entry represented. It was a gateway to the opportunities he had long envisioned, a chance to immerse himself in the culture of innovation that had captivated him from afar. His journey to Silicon Valley symbolized not just the achievement of a personal dream but the realization of a broader aspiration to contribute to the evolution of technology on a global scale.

This period in Yuan's life exemplifies the qualities that would later define his career: resilience, focus, and an unyielding commitment to his vision. The determination that carried him through nine rejections would become the foundation for his approach to innovation and leadership. Yuan's persistence in reaching Silicon Valley was not just a prelude to his future success but a lesson in the power of belief and tenacity. It was a defining moment that revealed the depth of his character and set the stage for the remarkable journey that lay ahead.

A New World: Joining WebEx
In 1997, Eric Yuan arrived in Silicon Valley, stepping into a world that was transforming at an unprecedented pace. The dot-com boom had reached its zenith, and the region buzzed with innovation, ambition, and the promise of a digital future. For a young engineer with a dream of contributing to groundbreaking projects, the timing was perfect. Silicon Valley was not just a place—it was an idea, a crucible where talent and technology converged to create the next big thing. Yuan, armed with determination and a willingness to learn, quickly found his footing in this dynamic environment. He secured a position at WebEx, a burgeoning company that was making waves in the field of web conferencing solutions.

At WebEx, Yuan became one of the company's early employees, a role that allowed him to delve deeply into the challenges and opportunities of building virtual communication tools. WebEx, though a rising star, was navigating uncharted territory as it sought to redefine how people connected remotely. Yuan was instrumental in the development of its core technology, dedicating himself to solving complex problems and improving the platform's capabilities. The work was demanding but rewarding, providing him with firsthand experience in crafting systems that could scale, adapt, and meet the needs of a diverse user base.

Beyond the technical aspects, Yuan's time at WebEx was marked by a growing awareness of the human side of communication technology. He worked closely with customers, often listening to their concerns and frustrations about the platform. These interactions provided him with a unique perspective on the user experience, highlighting the gap between what technology offered and what people actually needed. WebEx was undoubtedly a success, but it was not without its flaws. Users frequently expressed dissatisfaction with the platform's complexity, its unreliable connections, and its cumbersome interface. For Yuan, these complaints were more than just feedback—they were a challenge and an opportunity to envision something better.

Yuan's growing discontent with the limitations of WebEx planted the seeds of a vision that would later take shape as Zoom. He began to imagine a platform that could transcend the frustrations users faced, offering a seamless, intuitive, and reliable experience. His dissatisfaction was not born of cynicism but of a deep belief in the potential of communication technology to transform lives. He saw the possibility of creating a tool that not only facilitated meetings but made virtual interactions feel as natural as face-to-face conversations.

This period was also a time of intense learning for Yuan. He gained invaluable insights into the intricacies of communication technology, from the technical challenges of ensuring stability and scalability to the business dynamics of competing in a rapidly evolving market. He observed how decisions at the corporate level often prioritized immediate profitability over long-term user satisfaction, a trade-off that didn't sit well with him. Yuan's growing frustration with these compromises became a catalyst for his entrepreneurial aspirations. He began to believe that the only way to create the kind of product he envisioned was to build it himself, from the ground up, free from the constraints of existing corporate structures.

WebEx's success, coupled with its shortcomings, provided Yuan with a unique vantage point. He understood the potential of communication technology and the limitations that held it back. This duality of experience—success tempered by dissatisfaction—became a driving force in his career. It was during these years that Yuan developed the conviction that technology should serve people in the simplest, most effective way possible. He believed that the role of innovation was not just to meet technical requirements but to create meaningful and positive experiences for users.

Yuan's time at WebEx was transformative, shaping both his technical expertise and his vision for the future. It was a crucible of growth, where he honed his skills, deepened his understanding of user needs, and began to dream of a platform that could redefine virtual communication. While WebEx provided the foundation of his career in technology, it was also the place where Yuan realized the limitations of the existing approach and the immense potential for improvement. This realization would later become the cornerstone of his journey to create Zoom—a platform that would embody his belief in simplicity, reliability, and the power of human connection.

A Conflict of Visions: The Cisco Years

In 2007, WebEx was acquired by Cisco Systems, a major shift that would change not only the trajectory of the company but also the course of Eric Yuan's career. Cisco, a tech giant with a diverse portfolio and a strong foothold in the enterprise space, brought with it a new set of priorities. While the acquisition offered WebEx access to greater resources and a larger customer base, it also introduced new challenges—especially for Yuan, who had always been focused on creating a product that was intuitive and user-friendly. As part of Cisco, WebEx's focus began to shift more definitively toward serving large enterprise clients, whose needs and demands were different from those of individual users or small businesses.

Yuan, who had always been driven by a deep commitment to improving the user experience, found himself at odds with this shift. WebEx, now part of a vast corporate structure, had become more complex and less flexible in terms of innovation. As the platform began to cater more to corporate clients, it prioritized features that appealed to large organizations, such as advanced enterprise integration and security protocols, rather than simplifying the user interface or enhancing the reliability of the platform. Users' frustration with these issues, such as complicated setups and inconsistent connectivity, remained largely unaddressed. Yuan, acutely aware of these pain points, became a vocal advocate for change, proposing ideas that would make the platform more accessible, intuitive, and user-friendly. He suggested redesigns, streamlined processes, and a shift in focus to improve the overall user experience, believing that technology should serve people, not the other way around.

However, these suggestions were met with resistance. The corporate culture at Cisco, with its emphasis on large-scale enterprise solutions and its adherence to an existing business model, did not prioritize user-centric design. Yuan's vision, although grounded in his years of experience and understanding of user needs, was often dismissed or delayed in favor of the more traditional approach to business that Cisco was known for. This created a deep sense of frustration for Yuan, as he found himself unable to bring his ideas to life within the constraints of the corporate environment. The realization that he was fighting against a tide of institutional inertia made it clear to him that the changes he desired—those that could revolutionize communication technology—would not come from within a giant corporation like Cisco.

This period of frustration, however, was also enlightening for Yuan. It clarified his growing conviction that communication technology needed to focus primarily on user experience. He began to recognize that the existing solutions on the market, including WebEx, were not fulfilling their potential to make virtual communication simple, reliable, and enjoyable. More importantly, he understood that the technology industry, particularly in the realm of video conferencing, was evolving in ways that demanded innovation. The existing platforms were functional but lacked the sophistication and user-centered design that could transform the way people connected across distances. For Yuan, the moment of clarity came with the realization that if he wanted to create a truly transformative product, he could not do so within the confines of a large corporation that prioritized profitability over the human experience.

It was during this time that Yuan decided to leave his secure, high-ranking position at Cisco and pursue his vision independently. This was not a decision taken lightly, as it meant stepping away from the safety of a stable job at one of the world's leading tech companies. Yet Yuan's conviction that he could create something better was unwavering. He believed deeply that the opportunity to build a communication platform centered on the user experience was one worth pursuing, no matter the personal or professional risks. He also understood that to bring this vision to life, he would need to venture beyond the corporate structure and start from scratch, a daunting but exciting prospect.

Yuan's decision to leave Cisco marked a pivotal moment in his life. It was not just a career move; it was a bold step toward transforming the future of communication. He recognized that if he was going to create a platform that met the needs of real users—something that could work seamlessly, offer simple interfaces, and bridge the gap between people separated by distances—he needed to be in control of the process. He could not do this within a system that valued bureaucratic processes and slow innovation. Yuan's journey was about to take a new direction, one that would eventually lead him to create Zoom, a platform that would challenge the status quo and change the way the world communicated.

A Leap of Faith: Founding Zoom
In 2011, Yuan made the bold decision to leave Cisco and start his own venture. It was a risky move—he was entering a crowded market dominated by established players like Skype and Microsoft. Yuan's conviction, however, was unwavering. He believed there was a gap in the market for a product that combined simplicity, reliability, and scalability.

Yuan began assembling a team of like-minded engineers, many of whom were former colleagues who shared his vision. Operating on a tight budget, they worked tirelessly to develop what would become Zoom. From the beginning, Yuan's approach was hands-on and user-centric. He personally engaged with potential customers, gathering feedback to ensure that the platform addressed real-world needs.

Zoom's early development was guided by a singular principle: it had to "just work." Yuan and his team focused on creating a platform that was easy to use, fast to set up, and reliable under all conditions. They built a robust cloud-based infrastructure that could handle high volumes of traffic without compromising quality, a decision that would prove critical to the platform's success.

The team's dedication paid off when Zoom officially launched in 2013. It quickly gained a loyal following, thanks to its intuitive design and performance. Yuan's belief in listening to users and solving their problems became the cornerstone of Zoom's philosophy, setting it apart from competitors.

Eric Yuan's journey—from a small city in China to the heart of Silicon Valley—epitomizes the power of persistence, vision, and innovation. His story is not just about creating a product but about redefining an industry. By focusing on people rather than technology for its own sake, Yuan built a platform that has transformed how the world connects. As the subsequent chapters will reveal, Zoom's evolution into a global phenomenon was driven by this same commitment to making communication effortless and meaningful. Yuan's journey is a testament to the idea that great innovation often begins with a simple, human desire: the need to connect.

Chapter 2:
The Birth of Zoom

In the fast-paced and competitive world of Silicon Valley, where success often hinges on the ability to innovate rather than imitate, Eric Yuan's journey stands as a testament to vision and perseverance. In 2011, Yuan found himself at a critical juncture. After over a decade with WebEx, a pioneering company in video conferencing, he had grown increasingly disillusioned with its trajectory. The acquisition of WebEx by Cisco had brought corporate constraints, steering the company's focus away from user experience and innovation toward enterprise-driven goals. For Yuan, this shift stifled his creative instincts and clashed with his belief in technology as a means to empower users. He recognized that the video conferencing tools of the time were plagued by issues—complexity, unreliability, and user frustration were rampant. Yuan envisioned something radically different: a tool that was seamless, intuitive, and capable of truly connecting people in meaningful ways. With little more than a dream and an unshakable determination, he decided to leave Cisco and embark on a bold journey to bring his vision to life.

Leaving Stability Behind
Walking away from Cisco was a monumental decision for Eric Yuan, one that required both courage and conviction. At the time, he held a secure and lucrative position within a company that had a long history of success in the video conferencing space. He had played a key role in WebEx's growth and its eventual acquisition by Cisco, which solidified his standing in the tech industry. Yet, despite the security and prestige that came with his role, Yuan felt a growing sense of dissatisfaction. The acquisition of WebEx by Cisco had changed the company's culture and shifted its priorities, moving away from the innovative, user-centered approach that had once been the driving force behind WebEx's success. Yuan found himself

increasingly constrained by corporate bureaucracy and a lack of focus on true innovation. This realization prompted him to take the bold step of leaving the comfort of his corporate role to venture into uncharted territory and create something of his own.

The risks Yuan faced in leaving Cisco were immense. He was stepping into a world of uncertainty, with no guarantee of success. Starting a company from scratch meant navigating the challenges of building a team, securing funding, and developing a product that would stand out in a highly competitive market. On top of that, he was entering a space dominated by established giants like Skype, Microsoft, and Google, all of which had vast resources, large user bases, and significant brand recognition. These companies had already developed their own video conferencing solutions, and the market appeared.

The first critical step in realizing Eric Yuan's vision for a new and innovative video conferencing platform was assembling a team that shared his passion for both technological excellence and user-centric design. Yuan understood that to succeed, he needed more than just skilled engineers; he needed individuals who believed in his mission and were willing to invest not only their time but also their faith in the idea that they could reshape how people communicated. Drawing from his extensive network, Yuan reached out to former colleagues from his time at WebEx, individuals who knew him well and understood his vision for the future of communication technology. These professionals had witnessed Yuan's leadership firsthand and recognized his unwavering commitment to making technology accessible, intuitive, and, most importantly, effective.

However, persuading talented engineers and developers to leave stable, well-established roles at reputable companies to join a startup was no small feat. The risks associated with such a move were considerable, especially in an industry where the majority of startups fail within their first few years. It meant walking away from the security of a paycheck, benefits, and career advancement opportunities, and stepping into an uncertain future with no guarantee of success. Yet, Yuan's ability to inspire others played a pivotal role in overcoming these challenges. His reputation as a visionary leader, someone who had helped build WebEx into a successful company, made him a compelling figure. Many of those he approached were drawn to his conviction and passion for revolutionizing the video conferencing industry. They saw the potential in his vision and were willing to take the leap of faith with him.

The team Yuan assembled wasn't just highly skilled; they were also deeply committed to the mission of creating something groundbreaking. These individuals didn't view their work as just a job; they saw it as an opportunity to make a significant impact on the world by changing how people communicated across distances. This shared sense of purpose became the driving force behind the early days of the startup, fueling long hours, countless iterations, and the overcoming of numerous technical and logistical challenges. With a strong foundation of trust and a common vision, Yuan and his team set to work on building a product that would redefine video communication. Their dedication to the mission, combined with their technical expertise, created the perfect environment for the transformative innovations that would eventually make Zoom the success it is today.

The early days of Zoom were defined by relentless effort, perseverance, and a constant battle against skepticism. Operating out of a modest office in San Jose, California, Eric Yuan and his small but dedicated team faced a series of challenges that tested their resolve. With limited resources and a shoestring budget, they worked tirelessly, often putting in long hours with no guarantee of success. Despite the immense pressure, the team remained focused on their vision, understanding that the path to creating a transformative product would require both patience and unwavering commitment.

One of the most pressing challenges they faced was securing funding. In an environment where many investors were skeptical of yet another player entering the highly competitive video conferencing space, convincing potential backers to take a chance on Zoom was no easy feat. The video conferencing market at the time was already dominated by industry giants like Skype, Microsoft, and Google, all of whom had deep pockets and massive user bases. Many questioned the need for another video conferencing tool, arguing that the market was already saturated with established players. The idea of creating a new platform seemed, to many, like a futile exercise in redundancy.

However, Yuan's unwavering belief in his vision kept the team moving forward. He understood that their success would not come from competing with these giants in the same way, but from offering something fundamentally different. Yuan was determined to create a product that stood apart from the rest—not through flashy marketing or aggressive sales tactics, but by delivering superior quality, reliability, and ease of use. He and his team were committed to making Zoom a product that users could rely on, a platform that would "just work" without the technical headaches and glitches that plagued other solutions.

Yuan's conviction and the team's collective focus on solving real user problems became the driving force behind the development of Zoom. They knew that the key to success lay in creating an experience that was intuitive, seamless, and—most importantly—reliable. Each feature, every line of code, was designed with the user in mind, reflecting Yuan's philosophy that the best technology is invisible. This relentless focus on quality, usability, and user experience allowed Zoom to differentiate itself from the competition and, despite the skepticism they faced, set the stage for the platform's eventual success.

From the outset, Eric Yuan and his team placed an unwavering focus on simplicity as the guiding principle for Zoom's design. Yuan's belief that technology should be "invisible" was not just about aesthetics—it was about ensuring that technology seamlessly integrated into users' lives and did not create unnecessary barriers. This philosophy permeated every decision made in the development of Zoom. The goal was to create a product that anyone could use with ease, regardless of their technical expertise. By stripping away complexities, Zoom became an intuitive tool that allowed users to join meetings, share screens, or collaborate with just a few clicks. In contrast to the many video conferencing platforms of the time, which often required users to download multiple plugins or navigate complex, feature-heavy menus, Zoom simplified the process. The platform's interface was clean and user-friendly, with no confusing options or unnecessary steps. Yuan believed that by making the technology effortless, users could focus on the experience itself, not on overcoming technical obstacles. This design approach was groundbreaking, especially for users frustrated with the cumbersome nature of existing tools, and it positioned Zoom as a unique offering in a crowded market.

Reliability was just as important as simplicity, and Yuan and his team understood that without it, the platform would fail to gain users' trust. In the world of video conferencing, reliability is paramount; even a slight interruption or technical issue can derail a meeting, frustrate participants, and ruin the user experience. Yuan recognized that the frequent issues plaguing other platforms—such as dropped connections, poor video quality, or frozen screens—were unacceptable and needed to be addressed. To tackle this challenge head-on, the team built Zoom on a solid, cloud-based infrastructure that was designed to handle high volumes of traffic without sacrificing performance. The infrastructure needed to be scalable, able to adapt to both small team calls and large webinars with thousands of participants. This was no small feat, as Zoom had to ensure that it could function reliably across various devices, operating systems, and internet connections.

But beyond infrastructure, Yuan and his engineers also focused on optimizing Zoom's core technologies—its video and audio algorithms. The team understood that ensuring high-quality communication wasn't just about providing a connection, but about delivering a smooth, seamless experience even in challenging conditions. Many existing platforms were prone to poor video and audio quality, especially in low-bandwidth environments, leading to pixelated images or garbled audio. Yuan's vision for Zoom was to overcome these issues and provide a clear, uninterrupted experience. By fine-tuning Zoom's algorithms, the team ensured that even users in rural areas or with slower internet connections could have a reliable and high-quality experience. This emphasis on reliability set Zoom apart from its competitors, especially in situations where other platforms might falter.

Furthermore, Yuan's commitment to building a reliable, user-friendly platform helped to establish a strong sense of trust between Zoom and its growing user base. Users began to see Zoom not just as another video conferencing tool, but as a platform that they could depend on for important meetings, business presentations, and even family gatherings. As Zoom's reputation for reliability spread, more and more people turned to it, appreciating its consistent performance. Yuan's team continuously refined the platform, responding to user feedback and implementing improvements that further solidified Zoom's place as a leader in the video conferencing space. Ultimately, the combination of simplicity and reliability became Zoom's signature features—two qualities that ensured the platform's success, making it a tool that both businesses and everyday users could trust and enjoy.

Zoom's scalability played a pivotal role in its success, allowing the platform to meet a broad spectrum of needs while maintaining consistent performance. Eric Yuan's vision for Zoom was not limited to small-scale meetings or personal conversations; he sought to create a tool capable of supporting everything from intimate one-on-one calls to large virtual events involving thousands of participants. This scalability was a fundamental design principle for the team from the beginning. Yuan recognized that businesses, educators, healthcare providers, and individuals alike would all benefit from a platform that could seamlessly adapt to their varying needs. Unlike many video conferencing tools that were either too simplistic for enterprise-level needs or too complicated for casual users, Zoom aimed to be a versatile solution that could cater to everyone. Whether it was a small team meeting, a lecture for hundreds of students, or a global conference with thousands of attendees, Zoom's infrastructure was built to scale without sacrificing quality. This adaptability made Zoom particularly appealing across different industries, attracting users from diverse sectors who required both reliability and flexibility in their communication tools.

The ability to scale up or down quickly without compromising performance was made possible by Zoom's cloud-based architecture. This infrastructure was engineered to handle high traffic volumes, ensuring that the platform could efficiently support both small, personal conversations and large, complex virtual events. As the world increasingly relied on digital platforms for work, education, and social connection, Zoom's ability to scale became one of its most significant competitive advantages. This flexibility allowed Zoom to expand its user base rapidly, serving everything from individual consumers to Fortune 500 companies. It provided a one-stop solution that worked across industries, enabling businesses to host everything from routine team meetings to important webinars, and schools to conduct virtual classrooms. It wasn't just a video conferencing tool; it became a platform that could serve any audience without compromising quality.

Securing funding in the early days was another major challenge for Yuan. Despite his clear vision and the promising potential of Zoom, the market for video conferencing tools was already flooded with established competitors such as Skype, Microsoft, and Google. Many investors were skeptical about backing another startup in a saturated field. They questioned whether a new entrant could ever hope to compete with industry giants, especially when the market already had entrenched players with massive resources. Yuan, however, was undeterred. His belief in the potential of Zoom and the team's ability to innovate and deliver a superior product fueled his persistence. After facing multiple rejections, Yuan finally secured seed funding from a group of investors who shared his confidence in the product. This crucial investment enabled the team to continue developing the platform, refine its features, and prepare for its eventual launch. Yuan's ability to convince investors to back his vision, despite the challenges, was a testament to his unwavering determination and strategic thinking.

When Zoom officially launched in 2013, it was met with immediate praise from early adopters. Users were impressed by the platform's reliability, ease of use, and high-quality performance. Unlike many competitors that relied on expensive advertising campaigns to push their products, Zoom's growth was largely driven by word-of-mouth recommendations. Users were so impressed with the seamless experience and intuitive interface that they couldn't help but share their positive experiences with others. Yuan's decision to focus on building a product that directly addressed real user problems rather than simply adding features for the sake of complexity paid off. Word spread quickly, and Zoom gained traction organically, allowing it to build a loyal and growing user base. This organic growth was a clear indicator that the platform was not only solving a problem but doing so in a way that genuinely resonated with its users.

Zoom's rapid rise was a direct result of Yuan's steadfast focus on creating a product that solved real-world problems while adhering to his core philosophy of putting users first. Yuan's hands-on leadership style was a key part of Zoom's culture. From the beginning, he made it a priority to engage directly with users, solicit feedback, and make adjustments based on their needs. This close relationship with users helped shape the product into one that was both intuitive and reliable, earning the trust of millions. Yuan's approach was a clear reflection of his belief that technology should empower and connect people, rather than frustrate them with unnecessary complications. Zoom's success was not just about its technical excellence; it was also about a company culture that was driven by empathy, a commitment to solving real problems, and a determination to make communication easier and more effective for everyone.

The story of Zoom's creation is one of vision, resilience, and the relentless pursuit of excellence. Yuan's journey from corporate dissatisfaction to entrepreneurial success demonstrates the transformative power of focusing on user needs and staying true to a bold idea. With Zoom, he not only redefined video communication but also proved that even in the most competitive environments, a commitment to simplicity and reliability can pave the way for extraordinary success.

Chapter 3:
Breaking into a Crowded Market

Zoom's entry into the competitive world of video communication was far from a quiet emergence. Instead, it represented a determined and calculated push into an industry already dominated by well-established players. In the early 2010s, the video conferencing space was crowded with giants such as Skype, Microsoft Teams, Google Hangouts, and Cisco's WebEx, all of which held significant market shares. These platforms had already ingrained themselves into both individual and enterprise communication habits, supported by their vast resources, extensive marketing efforts, and established reputations. For a new entrant like Zoom, which had little name recognition, limited financial resources, and a small team, breaking into this established landscape might have seemed like an insurmountable challenge. Yet, Eric Yuan and his team saw an opportunity in these crowded waters, identifying key gaps in the market and using a strategy that emphasized simplicity, quality, and inclusivity. Their ability to carve out a distinct niche is a testament to their innovative thinking and bold decisions.

Understanding the Gaps in the Market
Yuan and his team were acutely aware that directly competing with the dominant players in the video communication market would be an uphill battle. Established platforms like Skype, WebEx, and Microsoft Teams had already solidified their positions with substantial user bases and considerable resources. Skype, for instance, was widely regarded as the go-to platform for individual and small-scale video communication. It had already embedded itself into the daily communication habits of millions of users. On the other hand, enterprise solutions like WebEx and Microsoft Teams had become deeply integrated into corporate workflows, offering advanced features designed to cater to the needs of large

organizations. These platforms were not only backed by massive financial and marketing resources but also enjoyed the trust of businesses and individuals alike, creating a difficult environment for any newcomer to penetrate.

Given this landscape, Yuan understood that attempting to outdo these competitors on their terms would be an exercise in futility. Instead of trying to match or replicate what they had already achieved, Yuan chose a different approach. Rather than offering yet another version of the same product, he focused on identifying and addressing the fundamental weaknesses that users frequently complained about. While the market was flooded with video conferencing tools, Yuan saw a clear gap. Existing solutions, although functional, often fell short in critical areas that directly affected user experience. Common complaints included poor video and audio quality, frequent connection dropouts, confusing user interfaces, and general unreliability. These weren't just minor inconveniences; they were significant pain points that affected users on a daily basis, whether in personal meetings or business communications.

This insight became the bedrock of Zoom's strategy. Yuan didn't just want to create another tool that performed the same basic functions as the existing platforms; he aimed to create something that would transcend these issues and offer a significantly better user experience. His focus was clear: build a platform that was simple to use, reliable, and high-performing, with an emphasis on solving the problems users faced with existing services. He understood that users were not just looking for a platform to make video calls but for one that worked seamlessly, without the technical glitches, poor audio quality, or connection failures that were so common with other services. Yuan's vision was to design a product that would naturally attract users who were dissatisfied with the status quo.

By focusing on solving these core problems—poor quality, frequent disruptions, and complicated interfaces—Yuan and his team laid the foundation for Zoom's success. Rather than trying to compete head-to-head with established players in the market, Zoom's approach was to offer a product that was so simple, reliable, and intuitive that it would draw users away from the existing platforms, which often left much to be desired. This clear focus on real user needs, rather than on competing features or price points, would ultimately set Zoom apart from the crowded field and allow it to gain traction in the competitive video conferencing market.

Prioritizing User Experience
One of the most crucial decisions that Yuan and his team made in the early days of Zoom was their unwavering focus on user experience. Yuan had a fundamental belief that technology should make life easier, not more complicated. He understood that users didn't want to spend time grappling with technical issues or figuring out how to use the platform; they simply wanted to connect, communicate, and collaborate. This philosophy became the driving force behind every design and functionality choice for Zoom. Yuan and his team set out to create a platform that would be intuitive, seamless, and effortless for users, regardless of their technical background. They recognized that, at its core, video conferencing technology was meant to facilitate communication, not become a hurdle for users to overcome.

Unlike many of its competitors, Zoom was built with simplicity at its core. The platform's interface was clean and uncluttered, designed to provide users with everything they needed without overwhelming them with unnecessary features or distracting elements. This attention to user-friendly design meant that users could join or start a meeting without needing to navigate through complex menus or deal with convoluted processes. Even first-time users, who had never interacted with the platform before, could join a meeting with just a single click, making Zoom accessible and inviting to a wide range of people—from tech-savvy professionals to individuals with little technical expertise. This ease of use was one of Zoom's defining features, setting it apart from other video conferencing platforms that often required time-consuming installations or complicated login processes.

The decision to streamline the process of joining a meeting was not just a matter of design, but a strategic move to lower the barriers to entry for users. Yuan and his team wanted to ensure that Zoom could be used by anyone, regardless of their level of technical skill. They understood that the more friction there was in the process, the less likely users would be to adopt the platform, especially those who were already familiar with other video conferencing tools. By making the experience as simple and frictionless as possible, Zoom was able to attract a broad audience, from businesses looking for a reliable communication tool to casual users who just wanted an easy way to connect with family or friends.

This emphasis on simplicity wasn't just about design aesthetics; it was about creating a product that people could rely on without frustration. Yuan's vision was clear: to build a tool that would empower users, not confuse them. The result was a video conferencing platform that felt natural and intuitive, allowing users to focus on the content of their meetings rather than the technology behind them. This user-centered approach became a cornerstone of Zoom's success, laying the groundwork for its rapid adoption and widespread popularity.

Committing to Reliability
In addition to its focus on simplicity, reliability quickly became another essential pillar of Zoom's success. Yuan and his team were

acutely aware of the frustration users experienced with video conferencing platforms that were inconsistent, especially when dealing with high volumes of traffic or varying internet speeds. Many of Zoom's competitors struggled with issues like dropped calls, poor audio quality, and blurry video, particularly in environments where bandwidth was limited or fluctuated. These were not minor inconveniences; they were critical problems that could derail meetings and damage trust in a platform, especially in high-stakes scenarios like business conferences, educational sessions, or family gatherings. Yuan knew that for Zoom to be truly competitive, it needed to offer a solution that users could rely on, regardless of their internet connection or the number of participants.

To tackle this, Zoom's engineering team set out to build a robust backend infrastructure that could handle the demands of high-traffic environments while maintaining excellent performance. A key part of this strategy was the development of advanced algorithms designed to optimize both video and audio quality. These algorithms were specifically engineered to ensure smooth, high-quality communication even in low-bandwidth conditions. The team focused on reducing latency, preventing video buffering, and minimizing audio dropouts, all of which were common complaints for users of other platforms. This focus on reliability wasn't just a technical challenge; it was a strategic decision that directly contributed to Zoom's growing reputation as a dependable tool for both personal and professional use.

Yuan's understanding of the importance of reliability was rooted in his vision of creating a platform that users could trust in any situation. Whether it was a business meeting where every minute mattered, an online lecture that needed to go smoothly, or a personal video call to connect with loved ones across the world, Zoom had to work seamlessly. Yuan and his team worked tirelessly to ensure that Zoom could handle the stress of a wide range of use cases without compromising on performance. This attention to detail not only addressed the common technical issues that plagued other platforms but also helped build user trust—an essential factor in Zoom's long-term success.

The emphasis on reliability set Zoom apart in a crowded market, where many video conferencing platforms were often plagued by performance issues. While other tools might have offered feature-rich platforms, they frequently fell short when it came to dependable, high-quality performance. By addressing these pain points, Zoom positioned itself as a platform that users could count on, no matter the circumstances. As Zoom grew in popularity, its reputation for being both simple and reliable became a key selling point, contributing to its adoption by individuals, businesses, educational institutions, and healthcare providers. In a world where reliability is a critical factor in the success of any communication tool, Zoom's commitment to overcoming the common barriers of video conferencing was a game-changer.

The Power of a Free Tier
One of Zoom's most innovative and strategically bold decisions in its early days was the introduction of a free tier of service, a move that set it apart from many of its competitors in the video conferencing space. During a time when most platforms were focused on monetizing their services through paid subscription models, Zoom chose to prioritize user acquisition over immediate revenue. The free tier allowed users to host unlimited one-on-one meetings and group meetings lasting up to 40 minutes without any cost, a generous offering compared to many competitors who restricted functionality or charged for basic features.

This decision, while seemingly risky, was rooted in Yuan's long-term vision for Zoom. Offering a free plan meant taking on significant operational costs with no immediate return. However, Yuan believed that the key to success was building a large, engaged user base—one that could see the value of Zoom's high-quality, user-friendly platform. The free offering acted as an entry point, allowing individuals and small organizations to experience Zoom firsthand without the burden of subscription fees. This was especially appealing to small businesses, educational institutions, and non-profit organizations, many of whom were unable or unwilling to commit to expensive subscriptions with untested platforms. By providing these users with an opportunity to explore Zoom's ease of use and superior performance, Yuan knew they would likely become advocates for the platform once they experienced its benefits.

The success of the freemium model became evident as word-of-mouth recommendations began to spread. Users who had been impressed with Zoom's performance and simplicity were eager to share their positive experiences with friends, colleagues, and networks, driving organic growth. Many of these early users, having become familiar with the platform's capabilities, were more than willing to upgrade to paid plans for extended meeting durations, additional features, and increased participant limits. This created a viral effect, as the free tier acted as a gateway to Zoom's paid services, ultimately turning free users into paying customers over time.

This freemium model proved to be a game-changer for Zoom, helping the platform gain massive traction, particularly in its formative years when brand recognition was minimal, and competition was fierce. The ability to introduce users to the platform without the barrier of a subscription fee not only accelerated Zoom's growth but also solidified its reputation as a platform that was accessible and focused on delivering value to its users. Yuan's strategic decision to prioritize user acquisition over short-term profits paid off handsomely, enabling Zoom to build a loyal, satisfied user base that would propel the platform to become a global leader in video communication.

Fostering Inclusivity and Broad Appeal
Another key element that contributed significantly to Zoom's early growth was its unwavering commitment to inclusivity. While many of its competitors, such as WebEx and Microsoft Teams, were primarily focused on enterprise users and catered mostly to corporate environments, Zoom took a broader, more inclusive approach. Yuan and his team understood that video communication was not limited to business meetings alone; it had the potential to serve a much wider range of industries and needs. They recognized that sectors like education, healthcare, and personal communication all stood to benefit from an easy-to-use, reliable video conferencing tool.

Zoom's versatility quickly became one of its standout features. It wasn't just a solution for large corporations; it was a platform designed to be just as useful for small businesses, educators, healthcare providers, and even families. Small businesses could use it to hold team meetings, while universities could use it to host online classes or conduct remote learning sessions. Healthcare providers saw Zoom as a critical tool for telemedicine, enabling doctors to consult with patients remotely. Families, separated by distances, could use Zoom to stay connected with one another, sharing moments and maintaining relationships despite geographic barriers.

By making the platform accessible to such a diverse audience, Zoom tapped into markets that had been largely underserved by other video conferencing platforms. Unlike WebEx and Microsoft Teams, which primarily targeted corporate users, Zoom's broad appeal allowed it to establish a presence in industries ranging from education and healthcare to non-profit organizations and personal communication. This inclusivity was reflected not only in Zoom's product design but also in its pricing strategy, which made the platform accessible to both individuals and businesses of all sizes.

This broader market reach allowed Zoom to differentiate itself from its competitors, positioning itself as a solution that could scale to meet the needs of any user, regardless of industry or size. Yuan's team ensured that whether it was a small business or a large enterprise, a university or a healthcare provider, Zoom could meet the demands of diverse user groups. This adaptability became one of Zoom's defining characteristics and played a key role in its rapid growth, as users from all walks of life and industries saw it as a flexible, reliable, and cost-effective tool that could meet their communication needs. In doing so, Zoom carved out a niche that was not solely defined by the business world, further fueling its success across various sectors.

Strategic Marketing and Community Engagement
Although Zoom lacked the extensive advertising budgets that its larger competitors had, it cleverly leveraged other strategies to build its brand and expand its user base. One of the most powerful tools in Zoom's marketing arsenal was word-of-mouth. Yuan recognized early on that genuine user satisfaction and organic recommendations could be far more effective than expensive ad campaigns. As a result, he personally engaged with early adopters, actively seeking their feedback on the platform. This hands-on approach allowed Yuan and his team to refine and improve the product based on real user insights, ensuring that Zoom was not only functional but also aligned with the needs and preferences of its users.

This direct engagement also helped foster a strong sense of community and loyalty among users. Many early adopters appreciated Yuan's personal attention, and as they experienced firsthand the ease of use and reliability of Zoom, they became its most vocal advocates. This sense of connection and involvement with the development process helped solidify the platform's reputation as a user-friendly, customer-centric service, which further fueled its growth.

In addition to word-of-mouth marketing, Zoom capitalized on strategic partnerships with widely used tools such as Slack, Google Calendar, and Microsoft Outlook. These integrations were critical in increasing Zoom's accessibility and adoption. By embedding Zoom directly into the workflows of users already using these tools, Zoom was able to seamlessly integrate into their daily routines, making it easier to schedule and join meetings with just a few clicks. This level of convenience proved irresistible to many users, particularly those who already relied on these tools for communication and scheduling, making Zoom the logical choice for their video conferencing needs.

Through these grassroots efforts, Zoom built a strong reputation for being reliable, easy to use, and deeply integrated into the digital ecosystem many users already depended on. The strategic partnerships and organic growth from user recommendations helped Zoom to steadily build momentum, driving its adoption across a wide variety of sectors. As users found success with Zoom and shared their experiences, the platform's reputation grew, creating a snowball effect that attracted even more users. This approach not only allowed Zoom to overcome its lack of advertising resources but also established it as a trusted tool that was driven by user satisfaction and reliability.

As Zoom gained traction, the company continued to prioritize adaptability. Yuan maintained a relentless focus on listening to users and incorporating their feedback into the platform. New features were regularly rolled out, often in direct response to user requests, ensuring that Zoom stayed ahead of evolving user needs. This commitment to continuous improvement became a defining feature of Zoom's growth. In a competitive market where many platforms were slow to adapt, Zoom's ability to innovate quickly and maintain a customer-centric approach helped solidify its place as a leader in the space.

The challenges Zoom faced in breaking into an already saturated market were significant, but its unique approach allowed it to carve out a distinct niche. By prioritizing simplicity, reliability, and inclusivity, the company was able to attract users who were frustrated with existing platforms. Its freemium model, strategic partnerships, and commitment to customer feedback created a virtuous cycle of growth, with satisfied users driving further adoption. Yuan's vision and strategic decisions laid the foundation for Zoom to become a disruptive force in the world of video communication. In the years that followed, Zoom would continue to redefine the landscape of video communication, constantly adapting to meet the changing needs of its diverse user base.

Chapter 4:
The Rise of Zoom

The rise of Zoom is a story of relentless innovation, a deep understanding of user needs, and a marketing strategy that relied more on trust and organic adoption than aggressive campaigns. In the years following its launch in 2013, Zoom began to establish itself as more than just another video conferencing tool. It became a platform that redefined what virtual communication could be, setting new standards for reliability, user experience, and accessibility. At a time when the market for video communication was already crowded, Zoom managed to carve out a unique identity through its thoughtful features, seamless cross-platform functionality, and an uncanny ability to resonate with a diverse range of users. The platform's appeal went far beyond corporate boardrooms, finding a home in classrooms, healthcare facilities, social gatherings, and even personal relationships. As its popularity grew, Zoom's name became synonymous with video conferencing itself—a rare cultural milestone that reflected the profound impact it had on modern communication.

At the heart of Zoom's rise was its unwavering focus on innovation. From the very beginning, Eric Yuan and his team recognized that the key to standing out in a competitive landscape was to offer features and functionality that addressed real-world needs in ways no other platform could. While many competitors focused on adding layers of complexity to their offerings, Zoom took a different approach: it sought to simplify and enhance the core experience of connecting people. This philosophy was evident in the platform's early emphasis on high-definition video and audio quality. At a time when other services often struggled to deliver a smooth, uninterrupted experience, Zoom invested heavily in building a robust backend infrastructure that could handle high levels of traffic while maintaining exceptional performance. Its advanced compression algorithms ensured that meetings could proceed seamlessly even in low-bandwidth environments, a critical feature that earned the platform widespread praise.

Zoom's commitment to innovation extended beyond technical reliability to include features that fundamentally changed how people interacted in virtual spaces. One of the most groundbreaking additions was the introduction of breakout rooms, which allowed meeting hosts to divide participants into smaller, separate groups for discussions or collaborative activities. This feature was particularly popular among educators, who used it to replicate the dynamics of small group work in virtual classrooms. Businesses and organizations also found breakout rooms invaluable for brainstorming sessions, team-building exercises, and more intimate discussions during large meetings. The flexibility and ease with which hosts could create and manage these rooms set Zoom apart from its competitors, reinforcing its reputation as a platform designed with the user in mind.

Another key innovation was Zoom's commitment to cross-platform compatibility. Recognizing that users accessed virtual meetings from a variety of devices and operating systems, Zoom made it a priority to ensure a consistent experience across smartphones, tablets, desktops, and web browsers. This adaptability was crucial in making the platform accessible to a broad audience, from professionals logging in from office computers to students joining classes on mobile devices. The seamless integration of features across platforms not only enhanced usability but also positioned Zoom as a versatile tool that could meet the needs of virtually any user, regardless of their technological preferences or constraints. This universal accessibility became one of Zoom's defining characteristics, allowing it to reach a global audience with minimal friction.

Word-of-mouth marketing played a pivotal role in Zoom's gradual rise. Unlike many of its competitors, which relied heavily on expensive advertising campaigns and corporate partnerships, Zoom focused on letting its product speak for itself. Yuan and his team believed that the best way to grow the platform was to deliver an experience so compelling that users would naturally recommend it to others. This approach proved highly effective, as satisfied customers became enthusiastic advocates for the platform, sharing their positive experiences with colleagues, friends, and family. The freemium model also contributed to this organic growth, allowing individuals and small organizations to try the platform without any financial commitment. Once users experienced Zoom's superior quality and ease of use, many were more than willing to upgrade to paid plans for additional features. This strategy created a self-reinforcing cycle of adoption and loyalty, with new users joining the platform every day through personal recommendations and referrals.

As Zoom's user base expanded, so too did its cultural footprint. The term "Zoom Room" began to emerge as a shorthand for dedicated spaces, both physical and virtual, designed for Zoom meetings. In offices, schools, and homes around the world, people began setting up environments specifically tailored to optimize their Zoom experiences, complete with proper lighting, high-quality microphones, and professional backdrops. This phenomenon was a testament to the platform's impact on how people approached communication and productivity. The Zoom Room concept also reflected a broader cultural shift towards remote work and virtual interaction, trends that Zoom not only capitalized on but actively shaped.

The versatility of Zoom's features made it a platform that could adapt to an astonishing array of use cases. Businesses relied on Zoom for everything from team meetings to global conferences, appreciating its ability to scale effortlessly from one-on-one calls to events with thousands of participants. Educators used Zoom to transform the way they delivered lessons, leveraging tools like screen sharing, virtual whiteboards, and breakout rooms to create dynamic online classrooms. Healthcare providers adopted Zoom to facilitate telemedicine, connecting patients with doctors in ways that were both efficient and secure. Even casual users found value in the platform, using it to host virtual parties, family reunions, and social gatherings. This broad appeal was a major factor in Zoom's rise, allowing it to transcend the limitations of traditional video conferencing tools and establish itself as an essential part of daily life.

One of Zoom's most significant achievements during its rise was its ability to foster a sense of connection and intimacy in virtual spaces. While many other platforms felt impersonal and transactional, Zoom managed to create an environment where users could truly feel present with one another, even across great distances. This was no small feat, given the inherent challenges of replicating face-to-face interaction in a digital medium. Yet Zoom's emphasis on high-quality video and audio, combined with its intuitive interface, helped bridge the gap between physical and virtual presence. This ability to bring people closer together was particularly evident in the platform's use during major life events, from weddings and graduations to memorial services and holiday celebrations. In these moments, Zoom became more than just a tool; it became a lifeline, enabling people to share their most meaningful experiences despite physical separation.

As Zoom continued to grow, it maintained a relentless focus on listening to its users and adapting to their evolving needs. The company regularly sought feedback from its community, using insights from customers to refine existing features and develop new ones. This iterative approach to innovation ensured that Zoom remained at the forefront of the industry, consistently delivering value to its users while staying ahead of competitors. Yuan's leadership was instrumental in fostering this culture of continuous improvement. His hands-on approach and deep empathy for users set the tone for the entire organization, creating a company that was as responsive and dynamic as the platform it had built.

The rise of Zoom was not without its challenges, including the constant pressure to differentiate itself in a crowded market and the need to scale its infrastructure to meet growing demand. However, the company's ability to navigate these obstacles with agility and foresight was a testament to its strong foundation and clear vision. By the time Zoom emerged as a household name, it had already established itself as a leader in the video communication space, with a reputation for excellence that extended across industries and geographies. Its success was a reminder that even in the most competitive markets, there is always room for innovation, authenticity, and a genuine commitment to solving real problems.

Zoom's rise was not just a business success story; it was a cultural phenomenon that redefined how people connected in an increasingly digital world. Through its innovative features, user-centric design, and grassroots marketing efforts, Zoom managed to achieve what few other platforms had: it became indispensable. Whether facilitating global business operations, enabling remote education, or simply bringing people closer together, Zoom's impact was profound and far-reaching. Its journey from a fledgling startup to a global powerhouse is a testament to the power of vision, perseverance, and a deep understanding of what truly matters to users. The rise of Zoom is a story that continues to inspire, offering valuable lessons for anyone seeking to make a meaningful impact in the world of technology and beyond.

Chapter 5:
From Tool to Verb: The Pandemic Era

The COVID-19 pandemic was a moment of unprecedented disruption, and for Zoom, it was also an era of unparalleled opportunity and challenge. As the world came to a standstill in early 2020, entire industries, educational systems, and social lives were abruptly forced into virtual spaces. What had once been gradual trends toward remote work and online collaboration became immediate necessities, and Zoom found itself at the center of this transformation. In the months that followed, Zoom was no longer just a tool; it became a verb, a cultural touchstone that defined how people worked, learned, and stayed connected during a time of profound isolation. This chapter explores how Zoom became synonymous with video communication during the pandemic, the extraordinary pressures the company faced in scaling to meet explosive demand, and the wave of competitors that emerged in response to its success. It is a story of adaptation, resilience, and the double-edged sword of success during a global crisis.

Before the pandemic, Zoom had already begun to establish itself as a reliable and user-friendly platform for video communication, steadily building its user base through word-of-mouth recommendations and a reputation for simplicity and reliability. But even the most optimistic projections within the company could not have anticipated the seismic shift that would occur in early 2020. When countries around the world implemented lockdown measures to curb the spread of COVID-19, businesses were forced to adopt remote work models overnight, schools transitioned to online learning, and individuals sought ways to maintain social ties in a world where physical gatherings were no longer possible. Zoom, with its intuitive interface, robust feature set, and generous free tier, was uniquely positioned to meet these sudden and overwhelming needs. Within weeks, what had been a steadily growing platform became an essential lifeline for millions of people around the globe.

The numbers were staggering. In December 2019, Zoom had approximately 10 million daily meeting participants. By April 2020, that number had skyrocketed to over 300 million. This meteoric rise in usage presented extraordinary challenges for the company, particularly in terms of scaling its infrastructure to accommodate such unprecedented demand. Video communication is a resource-intensive process, requiring vast amounts of bandwidth, server capacity, and technical support to ensure a smooth user experience. For Zoom, the surge in users meant an immediate and dramatic increase in operational costs and logistical complexity. The company had to rapidly expand its server network, enhance its cybersecurity measures, and hire additional staff to handle the influx of new customers. These efforts required not only financial resources but also extraordinary coordination and agility, as the company raced to keep up with the demands of a world that now relied on its platform for everything from business meetings to birthday parties.

One of the defining characteristics of Zoom's response to the pandemic was its ability to adapt quickly to the needs of its users. As schools shifted to online learning, educators began using Zoom to conduct virtual classes, often for the first time. Recognizing the unique challenges of this transition, Zoom introduced new features tailored to the needs of teachers and students. These included virtual backgrounds to create a more professional or engaging classroom environment, enhanced security settings to prevent unauthorized access to meetings, and tools like polls and breakout rooms to facilitate interactive learning. The platform also lifted its 40-minute time limit for free accounts used by K-12 schools, a gesture that was widely praised and demonstrated the company's commitment to supporting education during the crisis.

At the same time, businesses of all sizes were grappling with the challenges of remote work. For many organizations, Zoom became the backbone of their operations, enabling teams to collaborate, hold client meetings, and maintain a sense of connection despite physical separation. The platform's reliability and ease of use made it an obvious choice for companies seeking to minimize disruptions to their workflows. Zoom's features, such as screen sharing, recording, and real-time transcription, proved invaluable for maintaining productivity in a remote environment. Large enterprises also relied on Zoom to host virtual conferences and webinars, events that had previously been conducted in person but were now reimagined for a digital format. These use cases highlighted Zoom's versatility and scalability, cementing its status as an indispensable tool for navigating the challenges of the pandemic.

The cultural impact of Zoom during this period was profound. The platform became a part of everyday language, with phrases like "Let's Zoom" or "Are you on a Zoom call?" entering the vernacular almost overnight. Virtual happy hours, family reunions, and even weddings and funerals were conducted on Zoom, illustrating its role in keeping people connected during a time of profound isolation. The platform became a symbol of resilience and adaptability, enabling people to maintain a sense of normalcy and community despite the physical barriers imposed by the pandemic. For many, Zoom was more than just a tool; it was a lifeline that helped them stay connected to their loved ones, their colleagues, and their sense of purpose during one of the most challenging periods in recent history.

However, Zoom's meteoric rise was not without its challenges and controversies. The rapid increase in users brought intense scrutiny to the platform's security and privacy practices. Incidents of "Zoombombing," in which unauthorized individuals disrupted meetings with inappropriate content, highlighted vulnerabilities in the platform's default settings. These incidents sparked widespread concern and criticism, prompting the company to take swift action to address the issues. Zoom implemented a series of updates to enhance security, including end-to-end encryption, password protection for meetings, and features to enable hosts to manage participants more effectively. While these measures helped restore confidence in the platform, they also underscored the challenges of scaling a technology at such an unprecedented pace.

The surge in demand for video communication during the pandemic also attracted a wave of new competitors and intensified competition from existing players. Tech giants like Microsoft, Google, and Facebook accelerated the development of their own video conferencing tools, adding new features and aggressively marketing their platforms. At the same time, smaller companies sought to carve out niches in specific markets, offering specialized solutions for education, healthcare, and other sectors. Despite this heightened competition, Zoom managed to maintain its leadership position, thanks to its strong brand recognition, loyal user base, and relentless focus on improving its product. The company continued to innovate, introducing new features like immersive virtual backgrounds, improved accessibility options, and integrations with other productivity tools. These efforts not only helped Zoom retain its existing users but also attracted new ones, ensuring its continued relevance in a rapidly evolving market.

The pandemic era also forced Zoom to confront the social and ethical implications of its newfound prominence. As the platform became a critical tool for governments, healthcare providers, and non-profit organizations, it played a vital role in addressing some of the most urgent challenges of the crisis. Telemedicine appointments conducted on Zoom allowed patients to receive medical care without exposing themselves to the risk of infection. Government agencies used the platform to coordinate emergency responses and communicate with the public. Non-profit organizations leveraged Zoom to provide support services, organize fundraisers, and advocate for vulnerable communities. These use cases highlighted the platform's potential to drive positive change, even in the face of adversity.

As the world began to emerge from the initial shock of the pandemic and adapt to a new normal, Zoom faced the challenge of sustaining its momentum and proving its value in a post-pandemic landscape. The company recognized that the habits and behaviors formed during the pandemic—such as remote work, online education, and virtual socializing—were likely to have lasting effects. Zoom positioned itself as a platform not just for crisis management but for the future of communication, with a vision of enabling seamless collaboration and connection across physical and digital spaces. This forward-looking approach ensured that Zoom remained at the forefront of innovation, even as the world transitioned to a hybrid model of in-person and virtual interaction.

The pandemic era was a defining chapter in Zoom's history, one that tested the company's resilience, adaptability, and commitment to its users. It was a period of extraordinary growth and profound impact, as Zoom became an essential part of daily life for millions of people around the world. The platform's rise from a tool to a verb was not just a reflection of its popularity but also a testament to its ability to meet the needs of a rapidly changing world. For Eric Yuan and his team, this era was both a validation of their vision and a reminder of the responsibility that comes with success. As Zoom continued to evolve and expand, it carried with it the lessons and experiences of this transformative period, shaping its future and its place in the world of communication.

Chapter 6:
Growing Pains

The extraordinary success Zoom experienced during the COVID-19 pandemic brought with it an inevitable wave of challenges, scrutiny, and growing pains. Initially designed as a business-focused video conferencing tool, Zoom quickly transformed into a ubiquitous platform used across multiple sectors, from work and education to social gatherings and healthcare. The company's rapid expansion, from millions of users to hundreds of millions almost overnight, exposed vulnerabilities that had been overlooked during its earlier stages. As Zoom became central to daily life for many, the platform faced an unprecedented level of attention, both positive and negative. This surge in usage, coupled with the diverse ways people were using the service, highlighted new challenges that Zoom had to address, including managing user concerns, ensuring security, and maintaining the trust that had fueled its meteoric rise.

One of the most significant challenges Zoom faced during this period was the emergence of "Zoom fatigue," a phenomenon that quickly became a widespread issue for users as video conferencing became an integral part of daily life. With the rapid shift to remote work, learning, and socializing, many individuals found themselves spending hours in virtual meetings each day. Unlike traditional in-person interactions, these virtual meetings came with unique demands that were mentally and physically taxing. For one, virtual meetings required participants to maintain an unnatural level of focus on their screens for prolonged periods, as there were no natural breaks, such as walking around or engaging in side conversations, to help ease the strain. Furthermore, the inability to pick up on non-verbal cues like body language and facial expressions, which are fundamental to in-person communication, added a layer of cognitive load to every interaction. Participants found themselves not only processing the content of the meeting but also constantly navigating the stress of self-monitoring, with the visibility of their own image throughout the session contributing to feelings of self-consciousness. These factors, combined with the limited opportunity for physical movement, led to widespread reports of fatigue, eye strain, and burnout. The collective complaints about Zoom fatigue highlighted the limitations of virtual communication, a tool that, while offering convenience, could not fully replicate the richness, nuance, and spontaneity of face-to-face interactions.

Recognizing the toll this was taking on users, Zoom took a number of steps to address and alleviate the issue of Zoom fatigue. One of the first changes was the introduction of a feature that allowed users to hide their own video feed during calls. This simple yet effective tool helped reduce the pressure of constantly observing oneself during virtual meetings, a source of stress for many. By enabling this option, Zoom provided users with a small but meaningful way to reclaim some level of comfort and privacy. In addition to this feature, Zoom also began to promote best practices for managing fatigue. The company encouraged users to schedule regular breaks between meetings, emphasizing the importance of stepping away from the screen to rest both eyes and mind. Zoom also recommended using audio-only modes when appropriate, particularly for less intense meetings, in order to reduce the cognitive load that came with constant visual engagement. These steps were part of Zoom's broader strategy to support healthy remote work practices, addressing the specific needs and concerns of its user base.

Beyond the technical adjustments, Zoom also sought to engage in wider conversations about the future of work and the broader implications of remote communication. As the pandemic reshaped how people interacted, Zoom positioned itself as not just a service provider but as a thought leader in the evolving landscape of digital communication. The company took a proactive interest in understanding and discussing the long-term effects of remote work, seeking to influence the way businesses and individuals thought about their digital interactions. Through webinars, blog posts, and partnerships, Zoom began to advocate for more mindful approaches to virtual communication, pushing for a balance between productivity and well-being in a world increasingly dependent on digital tools. These efforts demonstrated Zoom's commitment to addressing the challenges its platform created and reinforced its role as a leader in supporting users through the complexities of remote work and digital connection.

Another significant challenge that surfaced during Zoom's rapid rise was the issue of security and privacy, which became a focal point of concern as the platform's popularity skyrocketed. The sudden and massive surge in users brought with it an increased scrutiny of Zoom's safety protocols, particularly after a series of high-profile incidents of "Zoom-bombing." These intrusions involved uninvited participants disrupting meetings, often with offensive or inappropriate content, creating chaos in both professional and educational environments. The incidents were especially troubling in schools, where children and teachers were subjected to disturbing content during virtual classes. The media coverage surrounding these breaches was intense, with critics questioning whether Zoom, which had built its brand around reliability and ease of use, had adequately prepared for the scale of its rapid growth. As a result, Zoom found itself grappling with a security crisis that threatened to undermine its credibility and erode the trust it had earned from millions of users around the world.

In response to these mounting concerns, Zoom acted quickly to address the vulnerabilities in its platform. The company rolled out a suite of new security features designed to safeguard user privacy and prevent unwanted disruptions. Among these updates were default meeting passwords and the automatic activation of waiting rooms, which allowed meeting hosts to control who could join the session. Additionally, Zoom introduced end-to-end encryption for all users, a move that aimed to enhance the platform's security and reassure users that their conversations were being protected. These updates were part of a broader 90-day security plan that Zoom implemented in an effort to address the growing concerns and improve its platform's safety measures. The company's leadership, including CEO Eric Yuan, took a proactive approach, with Yuan personally addressing the public and offering an apology for the lapses. In his statement, Yuan took full responsibility for the breaches, promising that Zoom would take immediate action to prevent such incidents from occurring again in the future. The transparency and accountability displayed by Zoom during this crisis helped to reassure many users, signaling the company's commitment to regaining their trust.

Despite these swift and comprehensive actions, the security breaches had a lasting impact on Zoom's reputation. The incidents underscored the challenges that come with scaling a platform at an unprecedented rate, particularly when it comes to safeguarding user data and preventing security threats. The heightened scrutiny also made it clear that, in a world increasingly reliant on digital communication, robust security protocols were no longer optional but essential. Although Zoom's response helped to address immediate concerns and restore some level of user confidence, the security lapses served as a reminder of the importance of being prepared for the complexities of rapid expansion, especially in an era where privacy and data security are top priorities for users. The lessons learned from this period were crucial in shaping Zoom's approach to security going forward, and the company has continued to invest in strengthening its privacy measures to avoid similar issues in the future.

Beyond the immediate security threats, Zoom also faced intense scrutiny over its data privacy practices, particularly as its global presence expanded. A major concern arose when reports surfaced that Zoom had routed some calls through servers in China, raising fears of potential government surveillance and data breaches. The revelation ignited a firestorm of criticism, especially from users and regulatory bodies worried about the security of sensitive information being transmitted across international borders. Though Zoom clarified that the routing issue was an unintentional misconfiguration affecting a small subset of calls, the incident brought into sharp focus the challenges the company faced in managing user data across a global network. Given that Zoom had become an integral part of daily life for millions, particularly in education, business, and healthcare, the question of where and how user data was handled became more critical than ever.

The controversy surrounding Zoom's data routing practices highlighted the risks inherent in operating in politically sensitive regions, especially when it came to user privacy and compliance with local regulations. The incident raised broader questions about the company's ability to safeguard data and the potential for governmental interference in private communications. In particular, the idea of Chinese government oversight of data transmitted through servers located in China became a point of contention, with critics pointing out the lack of clarity around how Zoom would ensure the confidentiality of its users' information in such an environment. For many users, particularly in Western countries, these concerns touched on the larger issue of the balance between security, privacy, and the global nature of technology platforms.

In response to these concerns, Zoom took several important steps to reinforce its commitment to data privacy and security. First, the company tightened its data routing policies, ensuring that sensitive information would no longer be routed through China or other regions where it could potentially be subject to government surveillance. Zoom also increased transparency about its infrastructure and how user data was handled, making public the details of its servers and routing practices. In addition, the company engaged third-party experts to conduct independent audits of its security and data privacy practices, signaling its commitment to holding itself accountable to external scrutiny. These audits helped to ensure that Zoom was meeting the highest standards for data protection and privacy.

These actions were part of a broader effort to rebuild trust with its users, who had grown increasingly wary about the potential misuse of their personal information. While Zoom's response was aimed at alleviating concerns about government surveillance, it also demonstrated the company's recognition of the broader implications of its role as a global communication platform. By taking these steps to strengthen its privacy practices and increase transparency, Zoom sought to reassure its users that their data would be handled responsibly and securely, reinforcing its commitment to protecting user privacy in a time when digital communication had become more critical than ever. The incident ultimately highlighted the complexities of operating on a global scale and the responsibility tech companies bear in safeguarding user data across diverse regulatory environments.

As Zoom grappled with its internal and external challenges, it also faced increasing competition in the video conferencing market. The pandemic had created an environment ripe for innovation, and established tech giants like Microsoft, Google, and Cisco moved quickly to capitalize on the surge in demand for remote communication tools. Microsoft Teams, for instance, gained traction with its seamless integration into Office 365, making it particularly appealing to enterprise customers. Similarly, Google Meet and Cisco Webex expanded their features, increasing the competitive pressure on Zoom.

In addition to these major players, smaller startups entered the market with specialized solutions tailored to specific industries or use cases. To maintain its competitive edge, Zoom had to continue innovating, regularly rolling out new features and refining its user experience. This dual focus on addressing security issues while simultaneously advancing its platform's capabilities became central to Zoom's strategy during this period. The company needed to stay ahead of the competition while also ensuring that it could continue to meet the growing demands of its user base.

Despite the challenges it faced, Zoom managed to retain the loyalty of its core user base and even expand its reach into new markets. Much of this success can be attributed to Zoom's transparent and proactive communication with its users. The company understood that its success was deeply intertwined with user trust, and by openly addressing the challenges it faced, it helped to rebuild and reinforce that trust. Zoom's leadership recognized that, while mistakes were inevitable during such rapid growth, how those mistakes were handled would ultimately determine the company's reputation.

Through direct engagement with users and swift action on security issues, Zoom not only navigated a period of intense scrutiny but also solidified its position as a leader in the video conferencing space. The company's ability to adapt quickly to emerging challenges, while keeping users informed, set a new standard for accountability in the tech industry. As a result, Zoom emerged from its early growing pains stronger, with a clearer understanding of the responsibilities that come with operating on such a massive scale.

The growing pains Zoom experienced were not unique to the company but reflected broader challenges in the digital communication landscape. The issues of Zoom fatigue, security, and privacy were emblematic of the growing pains faced by many tech companies as they scaled rapidly in response to a global crisis. By confronting these challenges head-on, Zoom helped to shape the discourse around digital communication, providing valuable lessons for other companies operating in the tech space.

These experiences also contributed to setting new industry standards for video conferencing platforms. Zoom's efforts to improve security, transparency, and user well-being in response to feedback became a benchmark for others in the field. The company's ability to adapt to its growing pains highlighted the importance of resilience and the need for tech companies to prioritize ethical considerations and user-centric practices as they scale.

Zoom's journey through the challenges of its explosive growth during the COVID-19 pandemic serves as a powerful reminder of the complexities of scaling a global platform. The company's ability to address issues like Zoom fatigue, security, privacy, and competition while maintaining trust with its user base allowed it to emerge from this period stronger and more resilient. However, the challenges it faced also underscored the importance of continuous innovation, transparency, and a commitment to ethical practices. For Zoom, these growing pains were not just obstacles to overcome but opportunities for learning and improvement, setting the stage for continued success in the ever-evolving world of digital communication.

Chapter 7:
The Cultural Phenomenon

In a world suddenly turned upside down by the COVID-19 pandemic, Zoom transcended its origins as a business communication tool to become a global cultural phenomenon. Its journey from a relatively obscure platform to a household name was as much a story of innovation and necessity as it was of adaptability and ubiquity. The platform didn't just facilitate communication during an unprecedented crisis; it redefined how people connected, celebrated, mourned, and created in a world where physical presence was often impossible. As remote-first practices and virtual interactions became the norm, Zoom seamlessly integrated itself into both the lexicon and the daily lives of millions, evolving from a piece of software into a verb, a cultural symbol, and a linchpin of human interaction. This chapter delves into the transformative role Zoom played in weddings, funerals, concerts, conferences, and more, exploring how it reshaped communication norms and solidified its place as a cornerstone of 21st-century culture.

When the pandemic forced a reevaluation of traditional ceremonies, Zoom became an unexpected solution for some of life's most deeply personal and collective moments. Weddings, a quintessentially in-person celebration, were among the first major life events to be reimagined for the virtual world. Couples who had meticulously planned large gatherings suddenly found themselves confronting the stark reality of lockdowns and travel restrictions. For many, Zoom offered a way to salvage their big day. With a webcam and a stable internet connection, weddings were live-streamed to family members across the globe. Officiants conducted ceremonies from their living rooms, guests attended in formal attire from the waist up, and reception dances unfolded in pixelated squares of joy. While virtual weddings lacked the tactile warmth of traditional ceremonies, they brought new possibilities for inclusion, allowing distant relatives, friends, and even strangers to share in moments of love and commitment without the barriers of geography or cost. Zoom became a tool not only of necessity but of accessibility, making these milestones possible in ways previously unimaginable.

Funerals, too, underwent a profound transformation through Zoom, becoming deeply symbolic of how the platform facilitated connection in times of grief. For those who lost loved ones during the pandemic, the inability to gather and grieve collectively was one of the most painful aspects of an already devastating time. Zoom emerged as a space where families could honor and remember those they had lost, creating virtual memorial services that, while unconventional, provided much-needed solace and solidarity. Mourners joined calls from different time zones, sharing memories, prayers, and tears. The ability to record these services added another layer of meaning, offering a way to preserve tributes for future reflection. While the digital divide excluded some from participating in these ceremonies, for many, Zoom represented a vital bridge in a moment of overwhelming disconnection. It turned private grief into a shared, albeit virtual, experience, highlighting the platform's capacity to support emotional bonds even in the absence of physical proximity.

Beyond personal milestones, Zoom played an instrumental role in reshaping cultural and creative expressions. The arts, a sector heavily reliant on live, in-person experiences, faced immense challenges during the pandemic. Theaters went dark, concert venues shuttered, and galleries closed their doors. But creativity found a way to adapt, and Zoom became an unexpected stage. Musicians hosted virtual concerts, bringing live performances into the homes of their audiences. Actors performed plays and readings, with each cast member broadcasting from their own space, relying on Zoom's gallery view to simulate ensemble interactions. Visual artists conducted workshops and shared their creative processes in real time. These innovations not only sustained the arts during a period of profound disruption but also democratized access to cultural experiences. A concert ticket that might have been prohibitively expensive for some was now free or offered at a fraction of the cost, streamed directly to anyone with an internet connection. Zoom enabled a new kind of intimacy between artists and audiences, collapsing the distance between creator and consumer and fostering a shared sense of resilience and community.

Perhaps one of the most striking aspects of Zoom's cultural phenomenon was its ability to host large-scale events that had previously relied on physical venues and logistical coordination. Academic conferences, business expos, political conventions, and even global summits moved online, leveraging Zoom's scalability and flexibility to bring together participants from all corners of the world. What these events lost in face-to-face interaction, they gained in inclusivity and environmental sustainability. Attendees who might not have been able to afford travel expenses or time away from work could now participate with a click of a button. Panels and keynote addresses were recorded and archived, extending their reach beyond the constraints of time zones and schedules. While virtual conferences lacked the serendipity of hallway conversations and networking over coffee, they offered new forms of engagement through interactive Q&A sessions, breakout rooms, and chat features. Zoom's role in facilitating these events underscored its adaptability and cemented its status as an indispensable tool for collaboration and exchange in a globally interconnected world.

Zoom's impact on communication norms and the collective lexicon was equally profound. The platform introduced a new vocabulary, with phrases like "Zoom fatigue," "Zoom happy hour," and "Zoom-bombing" becoming commonplace. The word "Zoom" itself transcended its original meaning, evolving into a verb synonymous with video conferencing as a whole. This linguistic shift reflected not only the platform's dominance but also its integration into the fabric of daily life. People began to speak of "Zooming" as naturally as they would of calling or texting, a testament to the platform's cultural ubiquity. At the same time, the norms of virtual communication began to evolve, shaped by the constraints and opportunities of the medium. Camera angles, lighting, and virtual backgrounds became new forms of self-presentation, blending elements of professional etiquette with personal expression. The ability to mute and unmute oneself introduced new dynamics to conversations, while features like chat and reactions allowed for simultaneous layers of communication within a single meeting. These shifts underscored the ways in which technology shapes not only how we communicate but also how we perceive and engage with one another.

While Zoom's cultural ascent was remarkable, it was not without its complexities and criticisms. The platform's sudden omnipresence raised questions about digital fatigue, privacy, and the long-term implications of virtual interaction. Critics argued that while Zoom enabled connection, it also contributed to a sense of disconnection, as human relationships were filtered through screens and reduced to boxes on a grid. Others pointed to the inequities of the digital divide, noting that access to high-speed internet and compatible devices was far from universal. These tensions highlighted the dual nature of Zoom's impact: it was both a bridge and a barrier, a tool that enabled unprecedented connection while also exposing existing inequalities and creating new challenges.

Despite these complexities, Zoom's role as a cultural phenomenon during this period cannot be overstated. It was more than just a piece of software; it was a symbol of adaptation, resilience, and the human capacity to find connection in the face of adversity. From the most personal moments of love and loss to the grand stages of art and global collaboration, Zoom became a space where life continued to unfold, even when the world outside seemed to stand still. Its influence on the norms, language, and possibilities of communication will undoubtedly endure, shaping how we connect, create, and celebrate in the years to come. In its transformation from a business tool to a cultural icon, Zoom not only reflected the needs and aspirations of its time but also redefined what it means to be together in a digital age.

Chapter 8:
The Road to Innovation

As the world began to emerge from the confines of the COVID-19 pandemic, Zoom faced a pivotal moment in its journey. The extraordinary demand for video conferencing that had catapulted it to global prominence during the pandemic was gradually giving way to a more nuanced and hybrid reality. In this new world, where in-person and virtual interactions coexisted, Zoom needed to demonstrate that its meteoric rise was not a fluke tied to a singular crisis but rather the foundation for sustained innovation and relevance. This was a daunting challenge but also an extraordinary opportunity. The company, once known primarily as a tool for virtual meetings, now sought to redefine itself as a multifaceted platform that would shape the future of work, collaboration, and digital interaction. Through strategic expansions into new domains such as Zoom Apps, Zoom Events, and the integration of emerging technologies like artificial intelligence, Zoom began to craft a vision that extended far beyond its origins. This chapter delves into how Zoom embraced the challenge of innovation in a hybrid world, exploring its technological advancements, market strategies, and aspirations for transforming digital communication and collaboration.

The hybrid model of work, which blended in-office and remote environments, was one of the most significant shifts that emerged in the post-pandemic era. This shift presented both opportunities and challenges for Zoom. On one hand, hybrid work underscored the ongoing need for robust and flexible communication tools. On the other, it demanded a level of sophistication and versatility that went beyond traditional video conferencing. Zoom recognized early on that maintaining relevance in this landscape required more than incremental improvements to its core product; it required a reimagining of what the platform could offer. One of the most notable steps in this direction was the introduction of Zoom Apps, an initiative designed to transform Zoom from a standalone tool into an ecosystem. Zoom Apps allowed users to integrate third-party applications directly into their meetings, creating seamless workflows that enhanced productivity and engagement. Whether it was brainstorming on virtual whiteboards, managing tasks, or conducting polls, Zoom Apps offered a way to enrich the meeting experience and align it more closely with the diverse needs of users. This move not only added value to the platform but also positioned Zoom as a hub for innovation, fostering a vibrant ecosystem of developers and partners.

Another key pillar of Zoom's post-pandemic strategy was its foray into the world of virtual and hybrid events through the launch of Zoom Events. The pandemic had demonstrated the viability of large-scale virtual gatherings, but as in-person events began to resume, the challenge was to create a solution that could bridge the gap between physical and digital spaces. Zoom Events was designed to do just that. It offered a comprehensive suite of tools for planning, hosting, and managing events that ranged from small webinars to multi-day conferences with thousands of attendees. Features like customizable event hubs, ticketing, analytics, and networking opportunities allowed organizers to create immersive and engaging experiences that transcended the limitations of traditional formats. By catering to both fully virtual and hybrid events, Zoom Events underscored the company's commitment to adaptability and its recognition of the diverse ways in which people now interacted. This initiative not only expanded Zoom's reach into new markets but also reinforced its role as a pioneer in the evolving landscape of digital engagement.

Zoom's exploration of emerging technologies, particularly artificial intelligence, represented another significant frontier in its journey toward innovation. AI had long been a buzzword in the tech industry, but Zoom sought to move beyond the hype by integrating AI in ways that were both practical and transformative. One of the most impactful applications of AI was in enhancing the user experience through features like real-time transcription, language translation, and smart summarization of meetings. These capabilities addressed common pain points, such as language barriers and the challenge of keeping track of lengthy discussions, making meetings more accessible and efficient for diverse audiences. Beyond these user-facing features, Zoom also leveraged AI to optimize backend processes, from improving video and audio quality to detecting and mitigating potential security threats. This dual focus on user experience and operational excellence demonstrated Zoom's holistic approach to innovation, ensuring that the platform remained not only functional but also intuitive and secure.

The company's vision for the future extended beyond individual products and features to encompass a broader philosophy about the role of technology in human interaction. Eric Yuan, Zoom's founder and CEO, often spoke of his aspiration to create a platform that fostered meaningful connections and brought people closer together. This vision was particularly evident in Zoom's investments in virtual reality (VR) and augmented reality (AR), technologies that had the potential to redefine the very nature of digital interaction. While these technologies were still in their infancy, Zoom began experimenting with ways to incorporate immersive elements into its platform. Imagine a meeting where participants could interact with 3D models, simulate physical spaces, or collaborate on projects as if they were in the same room, regardless of their physical location. These possibilities hinted at a future where the lines between virtual and physical interactions would blur, creating new opportunities for collaboration, creativity, and connection.

Zoom's commitment to innovation was also evident in its approach to inclusivity and accessibility. The company recognized that as its platform became more central to work, education, and social life, it had a responsibility to ensure that it was usable by as many people as possible. This commitment was reflected in features like screen reader support, customizable interfaces, and enhanced accessibility settings for individuals with disabilities. By prioritizing inclusivity, Zoom not only expanded its user base but also reinforced its ethos of creating technology that served people, not the other way around.

The road to innovation was not without its challenges. As Zoom ventured into new domains, it faced intense competition from established players and emerging startups alike. Tech giants such as Microsoft, Google, and Cisco, each with their own video conferencing solutions, continued to innovate aggressively, leveraging their vast ecosystems and resources to challenge Zoom's dominance. At the same time, specialized platforms targeting niche markets began to gain traction, forcing Zoom to constantly evaluate and refine its strategies. Internally, the rapid pace of innovation posed its own set of challenges, from managing resources and scaling operations to maintaining a cohesive vision in the face of ever-changing market dynamics. Yet, these challenges also served as catalysts for growth, pushing Zoom to remain agile, customer-focused, and forward-thinking.

Zoom's journey in the post-pandemic era was a testament to its resilience and adaptability. While the unprecedented surge in demand during the pandemic had been a defining moment, it was the company's response to the shifting landscape of the hybrid world that truly demonstrated its capacity for innovation. By expanding into new domains, embracing emerging technologies, and articulating a bold vision for the future, Zoom positioned itself not just as a tool for the present but as a platform for the possibilities of tomorrow. Its story was no longer just about navigating a crisis; it was about shaping a new era of digital interaction, one defined by flexibility, inclusivity, and the boundless potential of human connection. As Zoom continued to evolve, it carried with it the lessons of its past, the ambition of its present, and the promise of a future where innovation and humanity walked hand in hand.

Chapter 9:
Challenges and Critiques

Zoom's rapid rise to prominence has been a remarkable story of innovation, resilience, and adaptability. However, like many companies that experience swift growth, especially in a transformative industry, Zoom has faced its share of challenges and critiques. The platform's widespread use during the COVID-19 pandemic, when it became a central tool for work, education, and personal communication, placed it under intense scrutiny from users, governments, competitors, and the media. As Zoom scaled rapidly, it encountered a variety of hurdles, ranging from privacy and security concerns to critiques about its corporate culture and business practices. Despite its successes, Zoom had to navigate an increasingly competitive and regulated environment while preserving its reputation and user trust. This section explores the controversies Zoom faced, how it responded to these challenges, and the lessons it offers for companies in the modern technology and innovation landscape.

Privacy and Data Security Concerns
One of the earliest and most significant challenges Zoom faced was related to privacy and data security. The platform's rapid growth in early 2020, triggered by the COVID-19 pandemic, thrust it into the global spotlight, leading to heightened scrutiny of its security measures. As millions of people relied on Zoom for work, education, and personal communication, concerns about its ability to protect user information and maintain service integrity became a central issue. The platform's sudden rise to prominence revealed how quickly vulnerabilities could be exposed when scaling up an online service. High-profile incidents of "Zoom-bombing," where uninvited users intruded into meetings with offensive or inappropriate content, highlighted the risks that accompanied Zoom's swift expansion. These disruptive intrusions were

particularly alarming for educational institutions, businesses, and other professional environments that relied on Zoom for sensitive communications. What started as a nuisance quickly became a larger security concern, as these disruptions illustrated vulnerabilities in the platform's ability to prevent unauthorized access to meetings. At the time, Zoom relied on users to manually implement security features such as setting passwords and enabling waiting rooms for each meeting, but this decentralized approach failed to prevent the growing number of malicious incidents.

As the frequency of Zoom-bombing escalated, it became evident that Zoom needed to strengthen its security measures. The company responded by making several key changes aimed at bolstering its defenses. One of the first major updates was to implement default meeting passwords, ensuring that every meeting had a layer of protection without requiring users to manually configure settings. In addition, Zoom made waiting rooms mandatory by default, so hosts could control who joined their meetings. Perhaps most notably, Zoom introduced end-to-end encryption for all users, a step that was meant to ensure the privacy of communications and make it harder for unauthorized individuals to intercept data. While these actions demonstrated a clear commitment to improving security and restoring user confidence, the initial wave of breaches had already left a significant mark on the platform's reputation. The company had to work hard to regain the trust of its users, as many had been affected by the disruptions. Although Zoom made strides in addressing the immediate security concerns, the damage caused by the security breaches underscored the importance of having robust and scalable security infrastructure in place from the outset.

Beyond the security incidents, privacy concerns extended to Zoom's data handling practices. Reports surfaced that Zoom had been sending user data to third-party companies without adequate disclosure or consent, raising alarms about transparency and accountability. The revelation that Zoom was collecting more data than users had anticipated prompted further scrutiny of its privacy policies. Additionally, Zoom faced criticism for allegedly misrepresenting the level of encryption it provided. The company had marketed its platform as offering end-to-end encryption, but it was later discovered that this was not entirely accurate. Instead of truly end-to-end encryption, the platform had only provided encryption in transit, meaning that data could potentially be accessed while it was being processed on Zoom's servers. This misrepresentation led to accusations of misleading advertising and raised serious concerns about the company's commitment to privacy and user protection. As a result, Zoom found itself under investigation by regulators, including the Federal Trade Commission (FTC) in the United States, which initiated an inquiry into its practices. The investigation culminated in a settlement, in which Zoom agreed to implement a comprehensive data security program and undergo regular audits to ensure compliance with privacy standards.

This episode was a stark reminder of the delicate balance that technology companies must maintain between ambitious growth and ethical responsibility. Zoom had to confront the reality that its rapid scaling had outpaced its security and privacy infrastructure. The company's initial missteps in handling user data and security threats underscored the importance of transparency and accountability, particularly as it became a central tool for communication during a global crisis. For Zoom, the incident was a wake-up call that forced it to reassess its approach to user privacy and data security. The company recognized that, in order to sustain its growth and maintain user trust, it needed to prioritize transparency, strengthen its security protocols, and be more forthcoming about its data handling practices. The lessons learned from these early security and privacy challenges would ultimately shape Zoom's future approach to user protection, ensuring that it could continue to scale responsibly while safeguarding its users' data and trust.

Navigating Global Expansion and Geopolitical Tensions
As Zoom became a global phenomenon, its rapid expansion into international markets introduced a host of challenges related to navigating diverse regulatory and cultural landscapes. With users across the world, Zoom was tasked with balancing business objectives, local laws, and ethical principles, all while maintaining its reputation as a user-centric platform. One of the most prominent challenges arose in China, where Zoom faced significant criticism for allegedly complying with government requests to suspend accounts and censor content. This situation brought the company's global business practices into sharp focus, as it was accused of making compromises in order to maintain access to the highly lucrative Chinese market.

The controversy stemmed from the company's actions in shutting down meetings related to politically sensitive topics, such as discussions surrounding Chinese dissidents and pro-democracy movements. These meetings were abruptly interrupted, with participants being disconnected and accounts being suspended. The censorship, which appeared to align with the Chinese government's strict control over digital content, raised serious concerns about Zoom's commitment to freedom of expression and its willingness to put profit over principles. Critics argued that Zoom's actions, in effect, supported the Chinese government's efforts to suppress dissent, prompting broader debates about the ethical responsibilities of technology companies operating in politically sensitive regions. Many saw Zoom's compliance with local government demands as a dangerous precedent, one that placed its business interests above human rights and the protection of free speech.

In response, Zoom defended its actions, stating that it was simply complying with Chinese regulations that required companies to restrict access to content deemed politically sensitive. The company argued that its decision to censor content was not driven by political motives, but by its commitment to adhering to local laws, which is a common practice for businesses operating in foreign markets. However, the incident highlighted the delicate balancing act that companies like Zoom face when they operate in regions where laws may conflict with broader ethical values. The situation underscored the complexities that arise when companies are forced to choose between respecting local laws and protecting fundamental rights such as free speech and the right to assemble.

This episode served as a reminder of the challenges technology companies encounter as they scale globally, particularly when it comes to maintaining a consistent ethical stance while adhering to the legal frameworks of different countries. For Zoom, the situation exposed the inherent tensions between its global ambitions and its responsibility to uphold values like transparency, human rights, and free speech. In navigating the Chinese market, Zoom was forced to confront the uncomfortable reality that, in some cases, compliance with local regulations might come at the cost of the ethical principles it espoused.

Ultimately, the controversy in China was a pivotal moment in Zoom's history, prompting the company to reexamine its approach to corporate responsibility in politically sensitive regions. It raised important questions about the extent to which technology companies should be willing to compromise on their values in order to gain access to international markets. The incident also brought into sharper focus the broader issue of how multinational corporations must navigate the complexities of different legal and cultural contexts while balancing ethical considerations with business objectives. Moving forward, Zoom—and other companies like it—must grapple with these challenges as they continue to grow and expand into new global markets, where each decision could have far-reaching implications for their reputation, user trust, and long-term sustainability.

Intensified Competition
One of the most significant challenges Zoom faced during its rise to prominence was the intensifying competition in the video conferencing space. Before the COVID-19 pandemic, Zoom was one of several players offering video communication services, but the sudden surge in demand for remote work, learning, and personal communication dramatically altered the competitive landscape. As businesses, educational institutions, and individuals flocked to online platforms, established tech giants like Microsoft, Google, and Cisco quickly ramped up their efforts to challenge Zoom's dominance. This influx of competition intensified the pressure on Zoom to innovate and differentiate itself, all while maintaining the momentum it had gained.

Microsoft Teams, for example, became a formidable competitor due to its seamless integration with the Microsoft Office 365 suite, which appealed to enterprise users who were already embedded within Microsoft's ecosystem. The ability to easily access tools like Word, Excel, and PowerPoint within the same platform as video conferencing made Teams an attractive choice for businesses looking for an all-in-one productivity solution. This integration gave Microsoft a distinct advantage, especially in the corporate world, where teams already relied heavily on Microsoft's software. As a result, Microsoft Teams quickly gained traction, with a growing user base that posed a direct challenge to Zoom's efforts to capture the enterprise market.

Google Meet also emerged as a key player in the space, leveraging its vast reach within Google's suite of applications. With millions of users already relying on tools like Gmail, Google Drive, and Google Calendar, Google Meet was able to tap into this pre-existing user base, providing a simple and convenient video conferencing option. Google's ability to integrate Meet into its broader ecosystem made it an attractive choice for users, particularly those who were already committed to Google's services. Similarly, Cisco Webex, a longstanding player in the enterprise video conferencing market, sought to expand its features and enhance its user experience in order to regain relevance in the face of Zoom's rapid rise. With its extensive resources, Cisco was able to aggressively compete with Zoom in both the corporate and education sectors.

In addition to these established players, a wave of startups entered the market, offering niche solutions that targeted specific industries or use cases. Some focused on healthcare, providing video conferencing tailored to telemedicine needs, while others catered to specific educational or creative industries, offering specialized tools and features. This fragmentation of the market posed further challenges for Zoom, as it had to differentiate itself not only from the likes of Microsoft and Google but also from a growing number of startups carving out their own space in the video communication ecosystem.

In response to this mounting competition, Zoom had no choice but to continue innovating and refining its user experience. The company introduced new features and enhancements designed to appeal to both individual users and enterprise customers. These included advanced collaboration tools, improved integrations with third-party applications, and features like breakout rooms and webinar capabilities that allowed Zoom to maintain its edge in a crowded market. Moreover, Zoom focused on maintaining the simplicity and reliability that had been its original selling points, ensuring that even as the platform evolved, it remained easy to use and accessible to people with varying levels of technical expertise.

The increased competition spurred both growth and creativity at Zoom, forcing the company to stay agile and continuously adapt to the changing needs of its users. However, it also highlighted the challenge of maintaining a leadership position in such a rapidly evolving market. As the video conferencing space became more saturated, Zoom had to navigate the delicate balance of pushing forward with new innovations while preserving the core values that had made it successful in the first place. The pressure to stay ahead of competitors, while still catering to the diverse needs of its user base, has been an ongoing challenge for Zoom, but it has also driven the company to refine its offerings and ensure it remains relevant in a fast-moving and increasingly competitive industry.

Corporate Culture and Organizational Challenges
As Zoom expanded rapidly, it also faced significant internal challenges related to corporate culture and the dynamics of managing such explosive growth. The surge in demand for its services during the pandemic placed immense pressure on nearly every aspect of the company. The increasing number of users, many of whom were relying on Zoom for critical work, education, and personal connections, strained the platform's infrastructure, technology, and customer support systems. Employees found themselves working tirelessly to ensure that the platform could handle the unprecedented surge in traffic, maintain high service levels, and quickly resolve technical issues. This intense workload led to reports of burnout within the company. Many workers faced exhaustion as they struggled to keep up with the rapid pace of change and the mounting demands on the platform.

At the same time, the company's internal culture was put to the test. Zoom's success came with the challenge of maintaining its core values while scaling at a breakneck pace. As the company hired new employees to meet its growing needs, Zoom had to manage the challenge of integrating new staff into an organization that was expanding so quickly. The demand for talent and the speed of hiring also made it harder for the company to maintain the close-knit, collaborative culture that had been one of its distinguishing features in its early years. This rapid expansion required Zoom to rethink its internal processes, employee support systems, and work-life balance initiatives to ensure that employees were able to maintain their productivity without sacrificing their well-being.

Zoom also came under scrutiny for its lack of diversity and inclusivity, particularly within its leadership and workforce. Critics pointed to the underrepresentation of women and minorities in key roles, especially in the higher ranks of the company. While Zoom was lauded for its innovation and market success, it faced questions about whether its leadership was reflective of the diverse user base it served. The lack of diversity in the upper echelons of the company raised concerns about how well Zoom was equipped to navigate complex global markets and adapt to the diverse needs of its customers. Many observers argued that a more inclusive leadership team, with broader perspectives, could have helped the company more effectively address the internal and external challenges it was facing.

In response to these criticisms, Zoom pledged to improve its diversity and inclusion initiatives. The company recognized the need to foster a more equitable and supportive workplace, one that could better reflect the values it espoused and the global nature of its user base. In 2020, Zoom took concrete steps to address these issues by publicly committing to increase diversity within its workforce and leadership. The company began to invest in initiatives aimed at creating more opportunities for women and underrepresented minorities, both in hiring and in leadership development programs. It also made efforts to improve employee training on issues such as unconscious bias and inclusive practices. However, the process of building a truly diverse and inclusive organization is complex and ongoing, and Zoom has faced challenges in ensuring that its initiatives lead to measurable and sustainable change.

The company's efforts to address these internal issues reflect its recognition of the importance of cultivating a more balanced organization. However, the journey toward achieving a truly inclusive and equitable workplace has been slow, with progress that is often difficult to quantify. As Zoom continues to evolve, it remains committed to addressing these challenges, but the results of these efforts will likely take time to fully materialize. The company's journey highlights the tension between rapid growth and the need to ensure that organizational culture and inclusivity are prioritized alongside technological innovation and market expansion. The challenges Zoom faced in maintaining a healthy corporate culture during its period of explosive growth offer valuable lessons for other fast-growing companies looking to balance growth with the need for a supportive, inclusive work environment.

Despite the numerous critiques and challenges it faced, Zoom's ability to listen to feedback and adapt has been one of its defining strengths. The company has consistently shown a willingness to acknowledge its mistakes, engage with stakeholders, and implement necessary changes. For instance, its swift response to privacy and security concerns, coupled with significant investments in enhancing its protocols, demonstrated its commitment to user safety. Similarly, its efforts to address employee burnout and improve its diversity and inclusion practices illustrated a broader focus on continuous improvement. While these actions cannot erase the negative impact of earlier missteps, they highlight Zoom's resilience and adaptability. The company's ability to learn from its experiences and make changes accordingly has allowed it to maintain its place as a leading player in the video conferencing industry.

Ultimately, the challenges Zoom faced reflect both the demands of its success and the heightened scrutiny that comes with operating in a transformative industry. As Zoom became synonymous with video communication, its decisions were subjected to public and regulatory evaluation. This level of visibility brings with it significant responsibilities, including protecting user data, fostering inclusivity, and navigating the complexities of global markets. Zoom's journey illustrates the importance of transparency, ethical leadership, and a customer-centric approach in navigating these challenges. While the company has not always succeeded in meeting these responsibilities, it has learned valuable lessons about balancing ambition with accountability.

Looking ahead, Zoom will undoubtedly continue to face new challenges as the technology landscape evolves. Innovation is inherently accompanied by scrutiny, particularly for companies operating at the intersection of technology and human interaction. However, Zoom's history of resilience and its commitment to its users suggest that the company is well-equipped to tackle these challenges. By staying true to its mission of fostering meaningful connections and prioritizing the needs of its users, Zoom has the potential to not only overcome future obstacles but also emerge stronger and more impactful. The story of Zoom is not just about the hurdles it has faced but also about how it has responded to them, positioning itself to continue shaping a more connected and collaborative world.

Chapter 10:
The Legacy of Zoom

Zoom's rise to prominence is a story that encapsulates the essence of modern technological innovation: the ability to anticipate human needs, meet them with elegant solutions, and scale rapidly to impact lives across the globe. Its legacy is not merely as a tool for video communication but as a cultural, economic, and social phenomenon that transformed how people interact in the 21st century. From empowering global businesses to reinventing education and redefining personal connections, Zoom's imprint on society is as broad as it is profound. This concluding reflection explores the platform's far-reaching influence, the opportunities it created, and the benchmarks it set for user-centric innovation while also considering its role in reshaping the collective experience of connectivity. In doing so, we come to understand why Zoom's story is not only about technology but about humanity and its infinite capacity to adapt, innovate, and connect.

At the heart of Zoom's legacy lies its extraordinary ability to simplify and democratize communication. Before its arrival, video conferencing was often seen as a clunky, unreliable solution reserved for tech-savvy users or large enterprises with sophisticated IT departments. By prioritizing ease of use and accessibility, Zoom revolutionized the way people approached online communication. Its clean interface, minimal setup requirements, and compatibility with various devices made it the go-to platform for users of all ages and technical abilities. This democratization was particularly significant in underserved regions and populations, where complex and expensive tools had previously excluded many from participating in the digital revolution. Zoom opened up a new realm of possibilities for small businesses, nonprofit organizations, educators, and individuals, leveling the playing field and proving that technology could empower rather than intimidate.

In the business world, Zoom's impact has been nothing short of transformative. For decades, organizations relied on face-to-face meetings, often incurring significant costs in terms of travel and logistics. Zoom disrupted this paradigm by proving that virtual meetings could be just as productive, if not more so, while eliminating geographical barriers. Startups in developing nations gained newfound access to international markets, pitching investors and collaborating with partners halfway around the world. At the same time, large corporations used Zoom to streamline operations across their global offices, reducing their environmental footprint and boosting efficiency. The concept of hybrid work, which blends remote and in-office environments, owes much of its feasibility to Zoom's capabilities. By enabling seamless collaboration across time zones and continents, the platform has redefined productivity and paved the way for more inclusive, flexible work cultures that prioritize outcomes over physical presence.

Education represents another domain where Zoom's influence has been both profound and lasting. The COVID-19 pandemic forced an abrupt shift to online learning, and Zoom quickly became synonymous with virtual classrooms. For millions of students and teachers worldwide, the platform served as the primary bridge between education and disruption. While this transition posed challenges—particularly for those lacking reliable internet or adequate resources—it also brought opportunities. Zoom's user-friendly design allowed educators to adapt quickly, using tools like screen sharing, breakout rooms, and recording features to create interactive and engaging lessons. Beyond formal education, the platform became a hub for lifelong learning, enabling universities, cultural institutions, and independent educators to reach global audiences. This democratization of knowledge fostered a new era of accessibility, empowering individuals to acquire skills and insights that might have previously been out of reach due to geographic or financial constraints.

Zoom's cultural impact is perhaps its most visible and resonant legacy. Few technologies achieve the status of becoming a cultural verb, but Zoom managed to embed itself into the global lexicon. Phrases like "Zoom fatigue" and "Let's Zoom" became commonplace, reflecting both the ubiquity of the platform and its profound integration into daily life. During the pandemic, Zoom transcended its role as a business tool to become a stage for life's most meaningful moments. From virtual weddings and funerals to holiday gatherings and birthday celebrations, the platform became a lifeline for millions seeking connection in a time of isolation. Artists and performers turned to Zoom for virtual concerts, comedy shows, and creative collaborations, showcasing the platform's versatility as a medium for expression. This cultural resonance underscored Zoom's role not just as a technology but as a facilitator of human connection, reminding the world of the enduring importance of relationships, even in the face of physical separation.

However, the legacy of Zoom is not without its complexities. The platform's meteoric rise brought with it significant scrutiny, particularly around issues of privacy, security, and ethical responsibility. Early incidents of "Zoom-bombing," where uninvited participants disrupted meetings, highlighted vulnerabilities in the platform's design and raised questions about its readiness for widespread adoption. Furthermore, controversies over data handling practices and compliance with local regulations revealed the challenges of operating a global service in an increasingly interconnected yet fragmented world. While Zoom addressed many of these concerns with swift updates, transparency efforts, and a commitment to user education, these challenges serve as a reminder of the responsibilities that accompany technological power. Zoom's journey offers a cautionary tale about the need for vigilance and accountability, particularly when dealing with sensitive user data and global audiences.

Competition has also shaped Zoom's legacy, as it faced intense pressure from established players like Microsoft Teams, Google Meet, and Cisco Webex, as well as emerging startups targeting niche markets. Despite this crowded landscape, Zoom consistently maintained its competitive edge by prioritizing innovation, user experience, and reliability. Its ability to anticipate user needs and introduce features such as virtual backgrounds, enhanced security, and seamless integrations with third-party apps set a high standard for the industry. This relentless focus on improving the product not only solidified Zoom's position as a market leader but also pushed its competitors to raise their own standards, driving progress across the entire sector.

Looking toward the future, Zoom's legacy will likely evolve as it continues to explore new frontiers. The company's investments in emerging technologies such as artificial intelligence, augmented reality, and virtual reality suggest a vision for even more immersive and dynamic communication experiences. Initiatives like Zoom Apps, Zoom Events, and integrations with workplace ecosystems point to an ambition to go beyond video conferencing and redefine how people interact in professional and social contexts. While these innovations hold immense promise, they also come with new ethical and practical considerations, from ensuring accessibility to addressing the societal implications of increasingly sophisticated virtual environments.

Ultimately, the story of Zoom is one of connection. In a world that often feels divided—by geography, ideology, or circumstance—Zoom demonstrated the power of technology to bring people together. Its legacy is a testament to the enduring human desire for communication and collaboration, as well as the transformative potential of tools designed with empathy and purpose. By breaking down barriers and fostering inclusivity, Zoom set a benchmark for what technology can achieve when it is guided by the needs of its users. As it continues to innovate and adapt, Zoom's influence will endure as a symbol of resilience, ingenuity, and the unyielding importance of staying connected in an ever-changing world.

Conclusion

Zoom's journey from a niche video conferencing tool to a global phenomenon during the COVID-19 pandemic is a story of remarkable success, rapid growth, and complex challenges. The company's ability to scale at an unprecedented rate to meet the demands of remote work, education, and socialization was a testament to the power of technology in connecting people across vast distances. However, this rapid expansion also laid bare vulnerabilities in areas like security, privacy, and corporate culture. As Zoom navigated a turbulent landscape of increased competition, heightened public scrutiny, and internal growing pains, it was forced to adapt and innovate in ways that few companies ever experience.

The challenges Zoom faced—ranging from security breaches to the phenomenon of Zoom fatigue—served as important lessons not just for the company itself, but for the tech industry as a whole. They highlighted the delicate balance between maintaining a commitment to user trust and privacy while scaling a service that serves millions of people in diverse settings. In addressing these issues head-on, Zoom demonstrated resilience, transparency, and a proactive approach to user concerns. Through its efforts to improve security, prioritize privacy, and foster a healthier work-life balance for its users, Zoom showed that it was not only a platform for digital communication but also a leader in shaping the future of remote interaction.

As Zoom continues to evolve, the lessons learned during its meteoric rise will undoubtedly serve as a foundation for its future growth. The company's ability to embrace change, confront its shortcomings, and improve its services will determine its long-term success in an increasingly competitive and ever-changing digital landscape. Ultimately, Zoom's story is one of transformation—both for the company itself and for the broader world of digital communication. It is a reminder that even in the face of unprecedented challenges, innovation, transparency, and adaptability can lead to growth, and that the real measure of success lies in how a company responds to adversity.

www.ingramcontent.com/pod-product-compliance
Lightning Source LLC
Chambersburg PA
CBHW071104240526
45469CB00006BD/2327